AF322707

Voices of Marginalized Gender

Editors

Dr. Zeenat N. Kashmiri
Associate Professor
Department of Zoology
Dada Ramchand Bakhru Sindhu Mahavidyalaya
Nagpur, Maharashtra, India

Dr. Leena B. Chandnani
Professor
Department of Languages
Dada Ramchand Bakhru Sindhu Mahavidyalaya
Nagpur Maharashtra, India

Contents

Sr. No.	Title of Chapter	Author(s)	Page No.
1	Social Theories in Connection with the Four Agents of Gender Specialization: Family, Education, Peer Groups, and Mass Media	: Roshani Mahajan and Abhay Mudgal	1
2	Review on Health disparities and Research priorities in LGBT community	: Vaishnavi M. Chaudhari, Bharti S. Anerao and Arti M. Chaudhari	8
3	Struggles of Transgenders in India	: Susmita A. Mandavgane	16
4	Social Problems of Transgender and Struggle for Legal Recognition	: Meenakshi V. Wasnik	25
5	Legal Recognition of Transgender in India: Current Status and Challenges	: Sonika Kochhar and Pooja Mohobe	35
6	False Representation of the Marginalized Gender by the Recent Bollywood and Tollywood	: Doyel Bhattacharya, Babita Yadao, Himani Pandhurnekar, Pooja Mohobe	44
7	Women Empowerment with Implementation of POSH Act 2013 of *"The Sexual Harassment of Women at Workplace"*	: Renuka L. Roy	51
8	The Fight Against Marital Abuse as Depicted in the Hollywood Movie *Provoked*	: Suman Keswani	57
9	Transgender and Women's Empowerment in India: A Historical and Cultural Perspective	: Sharda Bhagchandani 'Aashna' and Damini Motwani	63
10	Women, Caste and Reform	: Anshu Choudhary	69
11	Unheard Voices of the Relegated Mythological Female Characters	: Hritika L Hisaria	75
12	Transgender in India	: Bharti A. Palaspagar	80
13	चित्रा मुदगल के उपन्यास 'एक ज़मीन अपनी' में आधुनिक नारी की तस्वीर व उसका आत्मबोध	: सपना तिवारी	84

Editorial

"How important it is for us to recognize and celebrate our heroes and sheroes" - Maya Angelou

Well said that men of quality respect women's equality. An equal world is an empowered world where every voice and every gender have equal rights. If gender equality is a human fight and not a gender fight then why do some members of human society experience marginalisation due to their gender?

Status enjoyed by the women in a society determines the very degree of civilization and extent of democratic setup. It is commonly agreed that the nature of the social organization, the degree of its civilization, and the amount of fair play and justice can be measured by the status enjoyed by women in that social organization. Three images of women in particular recur in the Indian scenario. They are Sita, Shakuntala and Savitri. These three women characters have come to symbolize the ideal of Indian womanhood and most of the female figures have been molded and fashioned after them. Incidentally, these images also reflect the man-woman relationship in society in that they imply an unquestionable superiority of man cast in the role of the protector of a weak and passive companion.

The positive side is that the Western culture, education, freedom struggle of the country and the changes in economic conditions proved powerful to bring the women out of the shadow of

Sita, Shakuntala and Savitri image. With the passing of the time the Indian woman has gradually come out of the cocoon of pride in suffering and has started looking at herself as a human being. This approach has evoked in her the germ of realization of 'herself' from all angles. The contemporary woman is torn between two antagonistic identities: her culturally conditioned sense of herself as a woman and her feministic aspirations for autonomy and selfhood. One of the most fundamental and far-reaching social changes accomplished in the evolution of Indian women is the emancipation from their traditional ethos.

However, her task of redefining her status as an individual was not an easy venture because of male dominance. If such difficulty was the path of the second gender how pathetic would be the journey of third gender. The transgenders have been marginalized and subject to discrimination. The theme of International Women 's Day 2024 is 'Inspire Inclusion' which means to truly include women and other genders to openly embrace their diversity of race, age, ability, faith, body image, and how they identify themselves. Worldwide these marginalised genders should be included in all fields of endeavour.

On 15 April 2014, in National Legal Services Authority v. Union of India, the Supreme Court of India ruled that transgender people should be treated as a third category of gender or as a socially and economically "backward" class entitled to proportional access and representation in education and jobs. The bill received presidential assent on 5 December 2019, following which the Ministry of Law and Justice published it in the Gazette of India as Act No. 40 of 2019. The act came into effect on 10 January 2020 after a notification of the same in the Gazette by the Ministry of Social Justice and Empowerment.

Women Empowerment Cell of the Dada Ramchand Bakhru Sindhu Mahavidyalaya, Nagpur is bringing its third edition *"Voices of Marginalized Gender"* which unfolds the feelings of not only subjugated women of Indian society but also the struggle for the identity of Transgender. The articles of this book dwell deep into the tangling and baffling struggles of these marginalized genders and fight and search for their identity in the male-dominated society.

The editorial board feel that this book will be useful to aspirant researchers and scholars who are working on gender equality and sensitization projects. This volume will certainly act as a torchbearer paving the way to changes in existing society and creating space in the community as well as hearts of people for the 2nd and 3rd genders making them walk parallel with the 1st gender.

"No one can make you feel inferior without your consent" - Eleanor Roosevelt

Editors

Acknowledgments

Women Empowerment Cell of Dada Ramchand Bakhru Sindhu Mahavidyalaya, Nagpur has published its third book titled ***"Voices of Marginalized Gender"***. The articles published in this book have been written on the given theme by faculty members from all across the state.

This book publication would not have been possible without many helping hands, whom the editorial board heartily wishes to thank.

We are extremely grateful to the hon'ble members of Sindhi Hindi Vidya Samiti, Nagpur, Dr. I. P. Keswani, President, Dr. Vinky Rughwani, Chairman, Mr. Neeraj Bakhru, General Secretary and Mr. Amit Bakhru, Secretary, College Affairs for always motivating and supporting us in our every endeavor. Our thanks are due to Principal Dr. V. M. Pendsey, Vice Principals, Dr. S.V. Tewani, Dr. M. M. Shinkhede and Dr. Mukesh Kaushik, and Dr. Y. V. Bhute, IQAC Coordinator for their inspiring words. We also acknowledge the painstaking efforts of our writers whose wonderful articles have helped us in framing our book.

We hope the publication of this volume will certainly furnish our readers with lots of knowledge and information.

We acknowledge the efforts of Ms. Aditi B. Chandanani for her contribution in cover page painting.

The team members of the Women Empowerment Cell have extended enthusiastic support by helping in compilation of the book and contributing their articles.

We are thankful to the Notion Press publisher for supporting us in the publication of this volume.

Editors

1. Social Theories in Connection with the Four Agents of Gender Specialization: Family, Education, Peer Groups, and Mass Media

Roshani Mahajan and Abhay Mudgal
VMV Commerce JMT Arts and JJP Science College, Nagpur
E-mail ID: roshani.mahajankatolkar@gmail.com; vmvabhay@gmail.com

Introduction

Gender socialization is a process by which one should develop and learn about the norms and roles as they interact with key agents of socialization, such as their family, education, peer group, and mass media. (Hoominfar, 2019, p.2)

From the very earliest period, the gender role was profoundly affected. The gender role (masculine and feminine) is one of the most important social topics in the 21st century. Many theories were propounded by the many authors to establish their views on gender studies. Due to globalization, gender roles have become a significant topic of discussion in today's era. According to sociologists, gender always shapes our behaviour, lives, and attitudes. It has a significant relationship with social class, sexuality, race, etc. Gender awareness is one of the most innovative research strategies. In society, it is common to notice that one should occupy a number of statuses simultaneously, like mother, daughter, son, employee, patient, and passenger. So, it is said that gender is presented as an emblem of family, community and society (Bal, 2016, p.7). Moreover, social norms always determine one's responsibility and privilege towards society. The idea that women's position is lower than men's is still prevalent in Indian society. Females are viewed as having a lower status both within and outside the house, which is linked to poorer status, less power, lower prestige, and lower or no compensation as compared to men. Due to their segregation into lower-paying occupations, women have fewer prospects for progression in their careers.

On the contrary, everyone is focused on gender equality in the wake of globalization, and women empowerment is perhaps a vital component for reaching gender equality, but in actuality, it is doomed to fail. Gender refers to the social, psychological and cultural traits that are connected to men and women in particular social contexts. Gender identity is acquired through learning, whereas sexual orientation is ascribed since it is innate. There is, however, one exception: regardless of their biological sex, certain cultures permit people to freely transition between genders. As we know, this is the reality or preoccupied thought that males always dominated female existence, However, the aforementioned claim is supported by Karl Marx's theory, which is predicated on the idea that society serves as a stage for the expression of power and dominance struggles. Marxist collaborator Friedrich Engels extended these presumptions to gender roles and the family. Engels said that a woman's household work is no longer valued in addition to a man's acquisition of basic needs. Women will only be able to achieve full independence when they are able to participate in large-scale social production and when domestic work only takes up a small portion of their time." (Lindsey, 2017, p.8).

Gender behaviour is determined by nature, which is based on biology, heredity, and genes. Sometimes it is also impacted by the environment and culture. It is a well-established fact that there are behavioral, mental, and sexual differences between men and women. For many years, the nature and nurture of humans have been simplified through the lenses of evaluation. Males and females have varied capacities due to genetics. Boys and girls are steered toward various life pathways due to heredity, and their gene also passes to the next generation, For example, the father consistently makes promises about his commitment to the family, while the mother is constantly flexible in caring for her kids. When we studied sex differences, we found that males are more aggressive than females. But sometimes girls also have an aggressive nature, but if a girl shows anger that is not supported by society in such a situation, she suppresses her anger and carries it out verbally.

Poverty and the oppression of racial and class groups are also linked to gender. It is seen that women are oppressed in society instead of being acknowledged for their privileges. There is various interdisciplinary research that is enrolled in academic programs like women's studies, gender studies, and men's studies. Which have wide scope in the future, so that gender studies become the prominent subject in literature to unfold the queries regarding gender inequality. Multicultural feminism, usually referred to as global feminism. It focuses on historical and cultural components that uphold the oppression of women. The women who were denied access to paid work, education, and health care due to their gender were given more authority thanks to the worldwide feminism movement. It also motivated women to use their own perceptions and experiences to avoid oppression lead by society. Sometime some political goals offer gender equality. Scholars argue that there is a significant difference between sex and gender. Sex refers to biological anatomy, and gender refers to the personal and psychological characteristics that society determines for women and men. Scholars argue that there is a significant difference between sex and gender. Sex refers to biological anatomy, and gender refers to the personal and psychological characteristics that society determines for women and men

There are numerous academics who contend that gender and sex are distinct concepts. Gender refers to the personal and psychological traits that society assigns to men and women, whereas sex relates to biological structure. (Hoominfar, 2019, p.3). These days, gender development is a crucial area of study that is backed by a lot of biological theories. According to essentialism males and females are fundamentally different from one another due to their biology and genetic makeup. And because of this, they are suitable for work irrespective of their backgrounds, specializations, motivations, and intelligence. Conversely, essentialists claim that culture imposes a stronger obstacle to equality than biological form. Another theory put forward by Sigmund Freud addresses the psychology of gender roles, such as the Electra and Oedipus complexes. He was the only theorist who talked about human psychology in detail. In his addition, he talks about five stages of psychosexual development (oral, anal, phallic, latency and genital). According to Freud Male children are attracted to their mothers, whereas female children are drawn to their fathers, for this is that the girl lacks a penis while the boy has one. The little girl's constant wish, motivated purely by "penis envy," is to be a boy. Because she lacks it too, she views her mother as inferior. The girl's *libido* or sexual energy is transferred to the father, who turns into her object of affection. Later Freud gave its name as *Electra Complex*. However, the girl's want for a penis is replaced with a wish for a child a few days later. A boy is even more appealing because he arrives with a much-desired penis. In contrast, a boy also goes through conflict when he is in the phallic stage of development. This is the time when his mother is the object of his libido and his father is the competitor for her love. This phenomenon was dubbed the Oedipus Complex by Freud. Freud asserts that the problem of dominion in human relationships is not because of social interaction but because of the individual psyche. The newborn baby is just like a blank slate on which gender identity will be written. It just like John Lock philosophy *"Tabula Rasa"*.

As a result of globalization, society gives preference to sexuality through the media. The people easily represent their views, opinions, and ideas regarding homosexuality and heterosexuality. To support this ideology, the queer theory came into existence in 1990. It looks at the social construction of sexuality and sexual identity in all of its manifestations, from sexual orientation to sexual desire. It divides sexual orientation into two categories, like homosexual and heterosexual. Homosexuals are people who have relationships with people of the same gender. Homosexual males referred to as gay men and homosexual females as lesbians. Those who are heterosexuals are attracted to people of the opposite gender sexually and prefer them for their erotic appeal. There is an additional category, which is bisexual. People in this category, whose sexual orientation is flexible, may respond sexually to either gender.

There is various agents of gender specialization like family, education, peer group and mass media. Functionalists point out that social integration may be endangered if these agents fail to perform their socializing tasks appropriately. Conflict theorists draw attention to the fact that various agents have differing degrees of power, which makes socialization beneficial for some groups but detrimental for others. These agents do not exist independently of one another and are often inconsistent in the gendered message they send. This all agents play an influential role in determining gender roles during primary socialization.

Now it is essential to find out the relationship between social theories and the four agents of gender specialization like family, education, peer groups and media.

Family

Family plays a pivotal role in gender development and identification. When a child is born into a family, the family puts forward rules and ideas about the girl infant and the boy infant. For example, the boy was wrapped in a blue blanket, and the girl was wrapped in a pink blanket. With their growing age, the girls are expected to play with dolls and tiny stoves, pretending to be cooking meals, and the boys are expected to play with guns and tanks, pretending to be soldiers. Gender-specific toys are a preference expressed by both parents and children. Parents attempt to explain the gender gap to their kids in this way. Socialization is a lifelong process. The family is the first institute for the child where they can learn about the culture and develop a sense of self. Important cultural components are passed down from one generation to the next through socialization. Family helps a child acquire necessary skills, especially language, accepted behaviour in society, awareness of education, etc. It is the family which sets the standards regarding gender role in children. Families always encourage their male children to have a strong attitude and their female children to have the required emotional attitude. In this way family is responsible for shaping the personality and self-esteem of the child.

Education

The second factor that is essential to gender specialization is education. Education is one's fundamental right. Families are, as is evident, the first institution from which children acquire their fundamental social knowledge. However, when a child reaches kindergarten and preschool, this process continues. Family life paves the way for education. In school, the students are rewarded for their excellence with prizes; this act helps them to be motivated. It was in the 18th century that the first call for gender equality in education was made. Through education, the girl becomes wise in their taking decisions. Even after marriage if the girl is educated, she is able to face any kind of circumstances easily. Literate mothers always become good supporters of their children rather than illiterate mothers. Undoubtedly, a girl's education has a significant and beneficial effect on society. The Indian government aims to promote equity and well-being in society through a number of development initiatives and educational programs. Education provides knowledge, and knowledge is a source of development. In society, there is a slogan: 'Educating a girl means educating a family'. This shows the clear connection between education and family development.

Peer Group

Children inherit the gender role model set by their family when they interact with their peer group. For young children, parents establish the initial relationships with peers. The two three-year-olds love playing with their playmate of the same age. Parents also don't make them part ways against their will. They knew full well that the children never feel content and at ease in the family unit only. This situation drastically changes when kids start school. Since All of the plays, games, and activities that take place in schools have a strong gender role component and play a significant part in socialization. This is also seen when brother and sister play together. It has been discovered that gender roles influence the preferences of both boy and female children. For example, boys want to play elaborate, competitive, and rule-governed games all the time, while girls prefer meaningful activities and occasionally prefer to play inside games while watching TV. Social learning theory and cognitive development emphasize how crucial peers are in fostering gender segregation in early childhood. (Linda, 2011, p.71). Peer group influence clearly increases during the course of the school day. When a boy cries in front of other boys, it becomes a source of ridicule for him and forces him to confront his morality. At this age, every boy attempts to project his masculinity.

Mass Media

As a tool for socialization, the media creates and incorporates gender stereotypes. It uses radio, newspapers, television, and the Internet to disseminate impersonal information to a large audience. Because the media constantly bombards us with messages about expectations and norms, it aids in socializing. A wide range of mass media, such as TV series, films, magazines, and popular music, have an impact on gender roles. Particularly strongly linked to traditional and stereotypical gender ideas is television. Youngsters always assume that whatever they see has something to do with reality and the truth. The medium by which social norms for behavior are established is television. If we give an example here, even in TV serials, women are assigned the role of housewives or portrayed as helpless women

References

- Bal G. (2016). *Contemporary gender issues identity*, Status and Empowerment. Rawat Publications.

- Evans M. (2009). *Gender and social theory*. Rawat Publications.
- Hoominfar E. (2021). Gender socialization. (pp.645-654). Springer Nature Switzerland AG 2019. https://doi.org/10.1007/978-3-319-70060-1_13-1.
- Lindsey, L. (2011). *Gender roles a sociological perspective*. PHI Learning Private Limited.

2. Review on Health disparities and Research priorities in LGBT community

Vaishnavi M. Chaudhari[1], Bharti S. Anerao[2], Arti M. Chaudhari[3]
Department of Bioengineering, DY Patil International University Akurdi, Pune
Department of Physics, Dada Ramchand Bakhru Sindhu Mahavidyalaya, Nagpur
Department of Physics, Yeshwant Mahavidyalaya, Wardha
*Corresponding author - E-mail: artichaudhari222@gmail.com

Introduction

Nowadays, Lesbian, gay, bisexual, and transgender (LGBT) individuals are an increasingly open, acknowledged, and visible part of society. The transgender population is diverse in gender identity, expression, and sexual orientation. Some transgender individuals have undergone medical interventions to alter their sexual anatomy and physiology, others wish to have such procedures in the future, and still others do not. This research paper addresses research on the issues and barriers in front of LGBT people. Specifically, it reviews the major challenges associated with LGBT populations and addresses solutions to create positive attitudes among homosexuals.

The phrase "lesbian, gay, bisexual, and transgender community" (or "LGBT community") refers to a broad group that are diverse with respect to gender, sexual orientation, race/ethnicity, and socioeconomic status. Homosexuality is defined as individuals who form sexual relationships with members of their own sex. It is sexual attraction, romantic attraction or sexual behavior between people of the same sex or gender [1]. It is perceived as abnormal and unacceptable by many people. Some homosexuals are ignored by their families due to social pressure, are fired from their new jobs, and are exposed to hostile behavior from society. Some of them even feel fear when they know they are homosexual. Negative attitudes and fear among homosexuals are because of might be they are not thinking about the human spirit, romance and love but they only focus on strict norms of sexual intercourse and not sharing their views about their lives [2]. Suicidal ideation and behavior along with substance abuse is clearly higher in homosexuals, for some unknown reason, one of them might be due to high-risk behavior and practices.

Psychosocial Implications

Anxiety, depression, and substance addiction are among the mental issues that sexual minorities are more likely to experience, the unfavorable views held by society, which contribute to social exclusion and a rise in psychological difficulties. There is an increased risk of STIs among members of the LGBT community. Pre-exposure prophylaxis (PrEP), one of the key prevention techniques, is emphasized in light of the prevalence of HIV/AIDS [3], HPV, and other STIs. Notable issues include hate crimes, sexual racism, and acts of violence directed towards the LGBT community. Members of the LGBT community who do not finish school or who live in poorer neighborhoods may experience more barriers in access to care and more negative health outcomes. Those in rural areas or areas with fewer LGBT people may feel less comfortable coming out, have less support from families and friends, and lack access to an LGBT community.

The review calls attention to the rising rates of violence, which are frequently caused by extreme religious beliefs, and it promotes a change in society that leads to acceptance and understanding. In order to address the issues experienced by sexual minorities, greater awareness, education, and public acceptance are necessary [4].

Social acceptance level

There have been significant global shifts in the dynamics of cultural attitudes regarding homosexuality and gay rights. The study includes a wide range of metrics by utilizing 2,000 data points from national and international surveys, such as the World Values Survey (WVS), Ipsos, Pew Global Attitudes Surveys, and the International Social Survey Program (ISSP). The information covers a wide range of subjects, such as opinions regarding same- gender sexual behavior, acceptance of gay rights in various contexts, and feelings of discrimination against the LGBTQA (lesbian, gay, bisexual, transgender, queer/questioning, asexual.) community. Notable results include the observation that 87% of countries worldwide are showing a trend toward greater acceptance of gay activity. Regional assessments, however, show more complex trends, with different acceptance rate trajectories seen in Europe and Latin America. While Southern European and former Communist republics show more varying views, Northwest European countries regularly rank highly in acceptance. It is essential to look at regional differences in views on homosexuality and gay rights in order to comprehend the complex forces at work. Regional variations might be a reflection of sociopolitical, cultural, and historical influences. The data highlights unique trends in European nations, indicating different degrees of acceptability. The split of Europe into those that were once communist and those that were not. Study shows that states that were once communists generally have less acceptance of LGBT rights, as seen by their lower acceptance scores and rankings. Attitudes are influenced by one's religious orientation. Muslim nations typically show lesser support for homosexuality and gay rights, whereas data from Roman Catholic and Orthodox nations are in consistent, with some showing less support than others. This emphasizes how religious customs affect the attitudes of society. The Gross National Product (GNP) per capita and the Human Development Index (HDI) are reliable indicators of acceptability. Developed European nations are generally more tolerant, highlighting the link between prosperity and progressive religious orientation. Muslim nations typically show lesser support for homosexuality and gay rights, whereas data from Roman Catholic and Orthodox nations are inconsistent, with some showing less support than others. This emphasizes how religious customs affect the attitudes of society. One important aspect affecting public opinion is the legal status of gay marriage [5]. The acceptance of homosexual marriage is often higher in countries that permit it. There are causation problems that need to be investigated further due of the reciprocal relationship between legal recognition and societal opinions. An additional layer of analysis is added to the intercontinental datasets by including non-European categories. Economic metrics like GNP per capita show how economic development plays a key role in promoting progressive views on homosexuality and remain powerful predictors of acceptance. Divergent views are influenced by geopolitical divisions, specifically the separation between European and non-European nations. The acceptance rate is generally lower in non-European nations, highlighting the significance of the geopolitical backdrop in influencing public perspectives.

It is consistently the case that younger generations have more welcoming views on homosexuality and LGBT rights. The generational divide highlights how gradually shifting social norms have an impact. A higher level of education is associated with a higher level of acceptance. Although the pattern is constant, the size of the variations differs between nations, suggesting that education interacts with contextual and cultural factors. Women typically possess views that are a little more welcoming than those of males. Nonetheless, disparities in gender are slight and fluctuate between nations. Aging effects are less likely to be the cause of adjustments in views than cohort effects, according to the analysis of within-cohort changes. Positive improvements among cohorts across nations point to changing social norms as opposed to perspective alterations that come naturally with aging. The examination of geographic and demographic differences offers a thorough grasp of the variables impacting perceptions of homosexuality and gay rights. Although younger, better-educated generations in economically developed regions are generally more accepting, subtle variations in patterns among nations are shaped by the interaction of geopolitics, religion, and legal recognition. Cohort impacts highlight how opinions in society are still changing and highlight how dynamic this cultural revolution is. The multidimensional analysis provides insightful information that politicians, scholars, and activists may use to promote inclusive societies and the opinions toward same-gender sex are influenced by individual-level factors such as age, gender, political beliefs, and educational attainment. Higher-educated people, women, and younger people typically have more optimistic attitudes. A nation's legal acknowledgment of LGBT rights, economic progress, and religious beliefs are all important variables. The regression analysis's findings shed light on the intricate interactions between contextual and individual factors that influence how society perceives homosexuality and gay rights.

According to the study, there may be more global acceptance of homosexuality as cultures advance and experience generational changes. The study examines how stressful childhood experiences affect sexual minorities and psychosocial factors that influence mental health issues within the LGBT population. Racial and ethnic disparities in mental health outcomes.

Efforts to overcome the situation

The decriminalization of Section 377 by the Supreme Court marks progress, but the LGBTQ community still faces challenges in achieving full societal acceptance. Attention is directed towards crucial issues encompassing awareness, rights, and the authentic validation of LGBTQ individuals. Emphasizing normalcy, the LGBTQ community primarily differs in how their bodies function, underscoring the importance of social acceptance that acknowledges each person's self-awareness. Key areas of focus include sociocultural obstacles, genuine affirmation, and variations in LGBTQ functioning. Respecting LGBTQ rights becomes pivotal for fostering equality and dignity. Statistical data in India provides insightful perspectives into the LGBTQ community, while research findings shed light on social, medical, and financial challenges [6]. Recommendations aim to address these issues and advance the overall well- being of the community. The abstract underscores the significance of every individual living with dignity. Examining the historical background of homosexuality emphasizes societal shifts, and the impact of Section 377, enacted in 1862, has been detrimental to the LGBTQ community, leading to rights denial and instances of brutality. Notable opposition to decriminalization in 2003 and 2013 was eventually overcome by a landmark ruling in 2017, safeguarding the right to openly express sexual orientation. CJI Dipak Mishra emphasizes the core idea of equality without discrimination. The justification for LGBTQ inclusion lies in its necessity for India's social and economic progress. Challenges encompass physical, health, socioeconomic, and emotional aspects, as detailed in Chatterjee Subhrajit's research on marginalization and exclusion. Recommendations extend to tackling violence and providing assistance to oppressed LGBTQ communities, with workshops proposed for educators, policymakers, and private companies. International human rights law underscores obligations to protect LGBTQ rights. The goal is to raise consciousness, stress genuine affirmation, and encourage decency. A comprehensive literature review covers economic development, admissions experiences, and homelessness. The LGBTQ abbreviation is explained, and the community, founded on principles of solidarity, diversity, and individualism, is recognized for its contributions to civil rights movements. Addressing real-life issues faced by the LGBTQ community requires confronting social norms, discrimination, ignorance, and psychological perceptions [7]. A range of ideas, including family support, educational reform, and awareness campaigns, is proposed to foster a more inclusive and understanding society.

In the context of the issues outlined above, the IOM was asked by the National Institutes of Health (NIH) to convene a Committee on Lesbian, Gay, Bisexual, and Transgender Health Issues and Research Gaps and Opportunities. The 17-member committee included experts from the fields of mental health, biostatistics, clinical medicine, adolescent health and development, aging, parenting, behavioral sciences, HIV research, demography, racial and ethnic disparities, and health services research. The study was supported entirely by NIH.

Conclusion

In conclusion, the topic "Problem and challenges of LGBT: Social Work Perspective" was selected with the intention of keeping it simple and understandable for readers. This topic was chosen because it's time to end making fun of and passing judgment on LGBT people while discussing the issues and struggles they face in real life encounter. LGBT people are excluded from all social events and functions, including events or sessions with an emphasis on societal development. As social workers, we have to be proactive in encouraging these individuals to take the lead and participate equally in all societal activities, since this will not only provide them more self-assurance but also enable them to feel more at ease interacting with others compared to there community members.

As social workers, we can lead workshops in which participants actively participate of LGBT, where we may speak with them directly about their problems and get suggestions for how to support them help in establishing a secure and welcoming atmosphere for them, as they are more knowledgeable about regardless or not we are able to grasp the fundamentals, they will always be greater than us.

References

1. Lynn D. Wardle (2007), "The Biological Causes and Consequences of Homosexual Behavioral and Their Relevance for Family Law Policies", 56(3), DePaul L. Rev. 997.

2. Herek, G.M., Capitanio, J.P (1996), "Some of my best friend: Intergroup contact, concealable stigma and heterosexuals, attitude toward gay men and lesbians", Personality and Social Psychology Bulletin, 22,412-424.

3. Nemoto T., Sausa LA., Operario D., Keatley J. (2006), "Need for HIV/AIDS education and intervention for MTF transgenders:

Responding to the challenge", Journal of Homosexuality, 51(1), 183–202.

4. Meyer IH. (1995), "Minority stress and mental health in gay men", Journal of Health & Social Behavior. 36(1),38–56.

5. Pompili M., Lester D., Forte A. (2014), Seretti ME., Erbuto D.," Bisexuality and suicide: a systematic review of the current literature", J Sex Med, 11, 1903-1913.

6. King M., Semlyen J., Tai SS., Killaspy H., Osborn D., et al. (2008) , "A systematic review of mental disorder, suicide, and deliberate self harm in lesbian, gay and bisexual people", BMC Psychiatry, 8, 70.

7. Cohler BJ., Hammack P.L. (2007), "The psychological world of the gay teenager: Social change, narrative, and "normality", Journal of Youth and Adolescence, 36(1), 47–59.

3. Struggles of Transgenders in India

Susmita A. Mandavgane
Department of Chemistry
D. R. B. Sindhu Mahavidyalaya, Nagpur
Email ID: susmitamandavgane@gmail.com

Introduction

Transgender persons experience homelessness from their childhood, when an individual reveals their gender identity in the family, the problem begins. They are ill-treated and abused by everyone in the family. This homelessness often leads to survival sex and begging. A major number of transgender persons are not living with their family members due to parental reactions and abuse when revealing their gender identity. These findings call our attention to providing shelter homes or alternative shelters for transgender persons to rescue them and reintegrate them into families. Further, they are confronted with a multitude of issues that require careful consideration and resolution.

From Indian mythology, Ardhanarishwar represents the intimate union of Shiv and Shakti and is a symbol of cosmic Androgyny. The earliest images of it go back to AD-35 to AD-60. Bramha failed to create beings who would together produce offspring and later die as he lacked the power to create women until Shiva appeared before him in the androgynous form of Ardhanarishwar, the male form fused with female. Duality was born after Ardhanarishwar separated into God and Goddess Ardhanarishwar concept is germane to all the classical dances of India. Kathakali is the best example of female impersonation in Indian performing arts. Female impersonators can certainly be described as human counterparts of Ardhanarishwar. They represent the perfect harmony of purush and prakriti, of strength and emotion.

Transgenders are considered as the "third gender" in India. This category includes transgender men and women, individuals with intersex variations, gender queer individuals, and those who identify with socio-cultural identities such as kinnar, hijra, aravani, and jogta. Transgender

Ardhanarishvara, 6th century; Government Museum, Jhalawar, Rajasthan, India

people frequently experience marginalization and isolation, which can result in substance misuse, mental health problems, and a diminished quality of life. The transgender community in India has endured a long history of social, economic, and political marginalization and discrimination. Many individuals perceive transgender people as aberrant or deviant, and they are subjected to physical, emotional, and sexual assault-related violence and abuse. Additionally, they encounter maltreatment and discrimination, notwithstanding the nation's advancements in diverse sectors.

A considerable number of occurrences remain unreported as a result of apprehension regarding potential accountability or the absence of legal validation. Various terminologies employed are:

1. **Androgyny**: the fusion or combination of masculine and feminine attributes.

2. **Transgender**: Individuals who identify or express their gender in a manner distinct from the sex that is allocated to them at birth.

3. **Transvestite**: An individual who finds enjoyment in donning garments that are predominantly associated with the opposite gender.

4. **Eunuch**: A male who underwent early castration, which can result in significant hormonal repercussions.

5. **Homosexual**: Individuals who are attracted to those of the same sex.

6. **Hermaphrodite**: Any individual or animal that naturally or abnormally possesses both male and female genital organs or characteristics.

7. **Imitator**: An individual who assumes the identity of another for fraudulent or entertainment purposes.

A significant proportion of the approximately 80% of transgender individuals in India who are not employed in begging or sex work are subjected to gender-based violence and maltreatment. The majority of transgender individuals have adversity in their youth and encounter significant obstacles each day. In addition to encountering discrimination in employment and education, obtaining identification documents such as passports and voter identification cards can be challenging. The 2011 Census estimates that there are 480,000 transgender individuals in the United States. Notwithstanding the enactment of the Transgender Persons (Protection of Rights) Act, 2019, which aimed to prohibit prejudice against transgender individuals in healthcare, employment, and education and to acknowledge their right to self-perceived gender identity, their harassment persists ceaselessly, encompassing activities of daily living and job hunting.

Misrepresentation and Stereotyping

The prevalence of societal stereotypes regarding transgender individuals restricts their access to healthcare, employment, and education. This prejudice starts from the birth and ends with their death. This not only results in the denial of equal access to essential social commodities, including housing, health care, employment, and education, but it also marginalizes transgender individuals and places them among the most vulnerable groups susceptible to social exclusion (Coates, 2010). Transgender people are compelled to vacate their residences and inhabit the streets due to the response of their primary caregiver towards their gender identity or sexual minority status (Castellanos, 2016). A significant proportion of the homeless population has experienced family turmoil, abuse, substance abuse within the family, and victimization at school and in the home (Kipke et al., 1997; Ray, 2006; Cochran et al., 2002; Corliss et al., 2011). The majority of transgender individuals opt to depart due to intolerable conditions (Hyde, 2005). Temporary housing may consist of sharing a residence with family or friends, entering a shelter or group home, or residing in an abandoned building, vehicle, or park (Wilson et al., 2020). The lack of utilization and access to essential services by this demographic can be attributed to systemic obstacles as well as apprehension regarding rejection and harassment (Shelton, 2015). Transgender individuals encounter numerous societal obstacles concerning the acceptance, comprehension, and awareness of their gender identity (McCann, 2021). Survival intercourse is frequently practiced by the homeless in return for food, shelter, and other fundamental necessities (Kattari, 2017). Transgender individuals are frequently marginalized in our society and rejected by their peers and families, which increases their vulnerability to homelessness and unemployment (Spicer, 2010). The issue of homelessness among the transgender community is gaining prominence in the eyes of society, as alarmists document elevated rates of homelessness in comparison to the heterosexual population (Mathews, 2019).

They are coerced into begging, performing sex labor, and going about their badhai work in order to survive. Further compounding these difficulties is the fact that transgender and GNC individuals face significant levels of discrimination when attempting to access social services, including mental health centers, drug treatment programs, rape crisis centers, and domestic violence shelters, and healthcare facilities such as emergency rooms, hospitals, and ambulances/EMTs. When endeavoring to access social services, numerous transgenders and GNC individuals have been subjected to anti-trans discrimination and outright denial of service-by-service providers. However, these disparate experiences have been quantified in very few research endeavors; transgender/GNC individuals are notably underrepresented in the scientific literature, especially in regard to homelessness. Complicating matters, instances of harassment and discrimination frequently result in increased substance abuse among transgender and GNC individuals, thereby intensifying the demand for specific social services within this population.

Gender segregation is another concerning aspect of numerous service providers, including the majority of homeless shelters and substance treatment programs. Transgender/GNC individuals who are seeking access to shelter and/or substance use treatment programs may be compelled to make a difficult decision: either accessing these services while assuming the identity of a gender they do not identify with, or failing to receive the necessary support. Numerous studies have demonstrated that in instances where transgender/GNC individuals choose to utilize homeless shelters, a significant number of these facilities fall short in terms of physically secure environments, privacy protection, and regard for the autonomy of transgender/GNC individuals as they define and express their gender identity. As a result of encountering discrimination in very institutions intended to assist them, transgender/GNC individuals may lack access to necessary services; consequently, many resort to survival sex in order to acquire resources and fundamental necessities. At some point, 10–50% of the homeless are estimated to have engaged in survival intercourse. Although frequently regarded as one of the few feasible alternatives for ensuring one's own survival and independence while living on the streets, survival sex has been associated with a multitude of negative consequences, such as increased likelihood of contracting and transmitting sexually transmitted infections (STIs), unintended pregnancies, substance use disorders, and suicidal thoughts and attempts. Nevertheless, it is crucial to acknowledge that although survival sex is resorted to by numerous individuals as their sole means of securing shelter, income, and safety, certain participants may perceive this as a financially empowering choice that enhances their own agency and may not perceive it as a completely detrimental consequence. Regarding the sample of transgender/GNC individuals, there is a paucity of research examining the associations between homelessness, survival sex, and other sociodemographic characteristics, irrespective of the motivations and/or oppressions that motivate homeless individuals to engage in this behavior. In this country, transgender people are subjected to physical, mental, and verbal harassment, in addition to being denied equal rights with people of the opposite gender. The United States is a nation that enthusiastically embraces diversity in religion, culture, and creed; in fact, our 'Unity in Diversity' motto is discussed internationally. However, the most abhorrent aspect of our culture is the unequal treatment of the sexes. Although all genders are regarded with respect under the law, there is still a social taboo regarding transgender individuals. Sadly, we live in a society where gender is a significant factor in evaluating individuals. Although transgender people are referred to as the "third gender," they are not permitted to coexist in peace and harmony.

The historical significance

Sociocultural groups comprising transgender individuals in our nation include hijras, jogtas, jogappas, Sakhis, and Aradhis. Every day, they are all subjected to severe discrimination and sexual harassment in every region of this country. These communities are not products of the last few centuries; in fact, they have existed for nearly four millennia since the beginning of time. Napunsaka is also mentioned in our Vedic literature, extending to the time of mythology. They are referred to in Jain literature as "psychological sex." Consequently, how did the notion of inequality originate in our nation? In 1871, during British rule, an act known as the "Criminal Tribes Act" was enacted, designating them as felons. This legislation significantly altered the national landscape. Despite the revocation of the law in 1949, transgender communities continued to face discrimination.

The primary obstacles encountered by the transgender community in India are as follows:

1) Discrimination in the workplace and educational institutions

A significant proportion of individuals within this community are uneducated or illiterate, limiting their ability to actively participate in the scholarly sphere. A census conducted in 2011 revealed that the transgender population numbered 4.9 lakhs, of which a mere 46% possessed literacy skills, a significantly lower rate than the 74% literacy rate observed in the general population. They are classified as a "disadvantaged group" under the Right to Education Act, which entitles them to a 25% reservation as an economically disadvantaged section. Their lower educational attainment can be attributed to factors such as poverty, social isolation from family and peers, and mental health challenges. The lack of access to educational opportunities exacerbates the difficulty of securing employment, and individuals who diligently pursue an education despite facing obstacles are not accorded equivalent regard and worth in the professional environment.

2) Homelessness and social exclusion

As a consequence of their limited access to education and employment opportunities, transgender communities are stigmatized and excluded from society. As a direct result of this exclusion, their self-esteem and self-confidence are severely damaged, and they ultimately accept undesirable employment. Due to abusive relationships that either evict them from their homes or prevent them from being embraced by their own families, they are deprived of a safe haven and a place to call home.

3) Coping Mechanisms for Transphobia and Psychological Anxiety

In contrast to individuals who identify as heterosexual, the transgender community encounters a greater degree of societal intolerance, harassment, and discrimination. As a consequence of societal, religious, and moral convictions, transphobic attitudes are uncommon; consequently, they do not inspire negativity, workplace harassment, or other forms of aggression. As a consequence of the aforementioned factors, the community is confronted with a multitude of mental health challenges, which may potentially precipitate adverse behaviors including self-harm and suicidal ideation. Loneliness, anxiety, and insecurities plague them as a result of societal influences.

4) Inadequate legal protection and susceptibility to hate crimes

The Transgender community faces a heightened vulnerability to hate crimes due to the limited legal protection it enjoys in comparison to other communities. They experience significant levels of violence and fall prey to hate crimes. Numerous police departments exhibit a lack of sensitivity towards these communities, to the extent that they fail to document the complaints lodged against them. Their subjugation at the hands of the police officers demonstrates our inefficiency as members of society.

5) The impact of media and stereotyping

The media frequently presents transgender individuals in a manner that is limited to insensitivity and stereotypical depictions. This type of portrayal serves to perpetuate unfavorable attitudes and further contributes to their maltreatment.

Conclusion

In conclusion, the transgender community comprises distinct sub-communities, namely hijras, jogtas, jogappas, Sakhis, and Aradhis, all of whom confront numerous obstacles in their daily lives. Social exclusion, marginalization, lack of education and employment opportunities, verbal abuse, sexual harassment, mental health issues, extreme poverty, violence, and victimization at the hands of hate crimes are some of these issues. The Transgender Protection Act, which was enacted in our nation, ensures that individuals of this nature are safeguarded against all forms of discrimination in employment, healthcare, and education. As members of the general public, it is our duty to treat them with the same regard and regard as any other gender. The multifaceted problem of transgender maltreatment in India stems from societal prejudices, legal loopholes, and economic inequalities.

Society can progress toward a future characterized by greater inclusivity and equity for all individuals, irrespective of their gender identity, by addressing the obstacles they face via legal reforms, communication networks, education, employment opportunities, healthcare access, and family support.

References

1. Coates J., McKenzie-Mohr S. (2010). Out of the frying pan, into the fire: Trauma in the lives of homeless youth prior to and during homelessness. *The Journal of Sociology & Social Welfare*, 37, 65.

2. Mottet L., Ohle J. (2006). Transitioning our shelters: Making homeless shelters safe for transgender people. *Journal of Poverty*, 10, 77–101.

3. National Alliance to End Homelessness. (2009). *Homeless youth and sexual exploitation: Research findings and practice implications.*

   Retrievedfrom http://www.endhomelessness.org/library/entry/homeless-youth-and-sexual-exploitation-research-findings-and-practice-impli.

4. Castellanos, H.D. (2016). The role of institutional placement, family conflict, and homosexuality in homelessness pathways among Latino LGBT youth in New York City. Journal of Homosexuality, 63(5), 601– 632.

5. Kattari, S.K. & Begun, S. (2017). On the Margins of Marginalized: Transgender Homelessness and Survival Sex. Affilia, 32(1), 92– 103.

6. Matthews, P., Poyner, C. & Kjellgren, R. (2019). Lesbian, gay, bisexual, transgender and queer experiences of homelessness and identity: insecurity and home (o) normativity. International Journal of Housing Policy, 19(2), 232-253.

7. McCann, E. & Brown, M.J. (2021). Homeless experiences and
    support needs of transgender people: A systematic review of
    the international evidence. Journal of nursing management,
    29(1), 85-94.

4. Social Problems of Transgender and Struggle for Legal Recognition

Meenakshi V. Wasnik
Department of English
Manoharrao Kamdi Mahavidyalaya, Nagpur
Email: mvwasnik@gmail.com

Introduction

Etymology of Transgender

The contemporary discourse on Transgender records that this community existed from way back in history. The existence of transgender people seems to be identified going back a thousand years ago. Their sense of self is undefined; their understanding of existence is unknown. In the concise and accessible introduction to Transgender, Chris Beasley provides a clear explanation of transgender as a term that "refers to those who reject their socially assigned gender and refuse to place themselves in the men and women gender binary." (Beasley, Chris 2005)

A closer look at getting recognition as transgender seems to be developed firstly as 'Transsexual' and later their recognition was developed as 'Transgender'. However, they are known by different names around the world. The Transgender are named as `Hijras' in India. The meaning of 'Hijra' as explicated in the most influential book *Me Hijra, Me Laxmi* authored by Tripathi, L. in which the meaning of `Hijra' is a term of abuse derived from Urdu, meaning "a person who has walked out of his tribe or community" (Tripathi, L. 2015)

The roots of transgender in India date back early since the Vedic period. Delli Swararao, K.in his paper "Hijras and their Social Life in South Asia." attempts to trace the aspects of the social identity of Transgender specially called as `Hijras' in South Asia. He states:

Hijras were once revered and accepted groups in Indian culture. The Vedas, ancient, Hindu texts include eunuchs and characters with both male and female characteristics. They were believed to bring luck and provide special fertility power. (Delli Swararao, K 2016)

Rights for Transgender constitute a set of norms that govern the ethical principle in terms of justice to transgender community and their way of life. These norms are incorporated into national and international legal systems, which specify mechanisms and create redressal cells to alleged victims of Transgender rights violations.

Many of the community are denied employment the moment they disclose their trans-identity. They are deprived of the right to participate in most economic activities. Even the most knowledgeable and eligible among the transgender people are denied in getting better positions in jobs. They are looked down upon in society in such a different way that they are left with no options to beg or pursue sex work. Owing to open sex work, this community faces significant health hazards.

Gender and sex constitute and influence a considerable portion of an individual's identity. While often used interchangeably in the past, it has presently come to denote completely different things altogether. Sex is the biological set up of a person, a combination of anatomical,endocrinal, and chromosomal features which make someone female and male. (Eckert & McConnell Ginet, 2013).

Zimmerman developed the definition of Gender. He states, "Gender, thus, is not something we are born with and not something we have, but something we do" (Zimmerman, 1978-1979). It is a system of roles and values assigned to the biological traits and functions that society has determined must align with what it considers the norm.

Historical Background of Transgender

The term 'transgender' was coined by John F. Oliven, a Psychiatrist of Columbia University, USA in his work 'Second Hygiene and Pathology' in the year 1965.

The community of trans-gender including trans-people till 1975 were considered under a single domain. Eventually, during the period of the 1990s and mid-2000s, these terms were used to denote female to male (FtM) for men who transitioned from female to male and male to female (MtF) for whoever transitioned from male to female. However, these terms are now obsolete. The terms Trans-men and Trans-women are seen to be applied to represent instead of (FtM) and (MtF) nowadays. There are marks of evidence in Ancient Indian History that acknowledge the recognition of the "third sex" of transgender.

The contributions, sacrifices, achievements, anger, and agony of Trans-genders are no less than the common people. The existence of Transgender spans since the great Indian epic like Mahabharata. It is from one of the Segments in Mahabharata that one could find the glimpse of the sacrifice of "transgender" where the transgender character *Shikahndi's* significance in the cause of the death of *Bhism Pitamah* cannot be devalued, underestimated or neglected.

The Mughal Ruling period is not far away to witness portrayal of this community in significant positions. The transgender in the arena of Mughal's are seen to hold the impressive responsibilities of political advisors, administrators, generals as well as guardians of the harems. In Arab Countries, the transgender are given high positions. In the religious institutions of Islam, they are seen placed in high positions specifically to safeguard the holy places of Mecca and Medina. They were considered trustworthy and also were the closest people to kings and queens.

M. Michelraj in his paper "Historical Evolution of Transgender Community in India '' attempts to focus on the evolution of the third sex in ancient Indian Texts. He explicates that "A third sex is also discussed in ancient Hindu law, medicine, linguistics and astrology." (Michel Raj, M. p.17)

Identity problems in Transgender

The experience of self-identity of Transgender can be observed in various ways. They come to know about their biological identity at any age. Transgender mostly recognizes their identity and feelings biologically from their earliest memories. Transgender people often experience forced or voluntary exile which leads to identity confusion and problems of identification. It is an inevitable fact that the transgender not only faces the biological dilemma but also face the social dilemma which is really very pitiful. Others recognize their transgender identities during adolescence or much later in life. Some are seen to embrace their transgender feelings, while others struggle with feelings of shame or confusion.

Lack of Security

The ways in which the Tran-genders have been conceptualized in terms of security and conflict have mostly been ambiguous. Economic insecurity, Social insecurity is common among Hijras or Trans-gender communities. Biological insecurity or say Biological identity is also one of the major factors influencing the economic and social insecurities in this community. The trans-genders do not expect support from their family background in the long run as they are often found evicted from home. Due to lack of support, they tend to experience a lot of challenges especially in terms of social recognition, Economic development and lack of employment opportunities or old age. Lack of livelihood is one of the major issues and concerns faced by Tans-genders. This compels them to work in any hazardous conditions related to their health issues affected with sexually transmitted Diseases like HIV. Few trans-genders have exceptional cases owing to their sporadic success stories of self-employed founders running some business or organizing cultural programs.

Role of Transgender in Social activism

In the theoretical debate, there is little research done on the subject of origin, scope and significance of rights to transgender in terms of politics, philosophy and jurisdiction owing to being a socially secluded part of the community. Modern Human Rights theory and practice found much of its scholarship for Tans-genders in Europe and North America that span around in 18th century French and American Revolutions. Likewise, this Human Rights theory and practice of Trans-gender further can be seen during the liberation of subjugated people from slavery and colonial domination in the 19th and 20th centuries.

In India, the transgender community is often discriminated against and harassed. To fight for the justice of these communities, some of the trans-activists are striving hard for their upliftment and empowerment. Among the Transgender rights activists in India, we find the famous name Laxmi Narayan Tripathi known as Laxmi is a Trans-gender rights activist, she is the Acharya Mahamandaleshwar of Kinnar Akhada.

Akkai Padmashali is yet another iconic figure in the names of trans-activists from South India. During the association with transgender people as a sex worker, Akkai Padmashali realized that the Government policies do not much favor their community.   Her persistent fight to remove the societal stigma in this community and to strengthen the people of this community made her found an organization called 'Ondede', meaning in Kannada is 'convergence.' The objective of Akkai's organization is to create sexual diversity, and to make people embrace the gender identity of their choice.

Controversies about Transgender Rights in Current Affairs

Rights to Transgender community can be understood globally only when an individual introspect how they are transformed from word to deed and from aspiration to practice. Transgenderism in the global context and in India is aptly explicated by Floyd, M., Martin, O., and Eckloff, K. J. They explored the true scenario of the transgender where these communities are considered as:

A stigma and a cloud of misunderstanding surround the concepts of both gender nonconformity and transgender. Even in the so-called 'first world countries', where transgenderism is not directly criminalized (unlike thirteen countries including United Arab Emi rates and   Indonesia), numerous obstacles are constructed that impede their daily experiences such as discrimination in the economy, offensive stereotype, inappropriate use of pronouns, and refusal of healthcare based on gender identity (Floyd, Martin, & Eckloff, 2019).

The Government of India passed the (Protection of Rights) Act, 2018 which gives rights and privileges to get employed and for the well-being of the transgender community.   Despite these Rights to Protection Act, the transgender community still continues to face challenges in their daily walks of life. Although the Supreme Court recognizes trans-genders as 'third gender', the existing social scenario still observes Gender Distinction in their personal, social and political life. These communities are still subject to discrimination in employment, educational institutes, and within families which severely affects their overall wellbeing.

The Government has passed the Transgender Persons (Protection of Rights) Act, 2019 that facilitates the transgender community to make their self-recognition and self-identity.

The Civil Society still visualizes this community as a Social Stigma as they often face difficulty in property inheritance or child adoption. Because of being socially subjugated, they are not even able to take up menial jobs. Owing to limited avenues of employment to transgender and severe discrimination, they are often found indulged into sex work.

Rights and Acts Provided for Transgender

NALSA Judgment

This case is marked as a milestone in the judgment of the National Legal Services Authority v. Union of India. This case endorsed the fundamental rights under the Constitution to get recognition to the person who falls outside the male or female gender binary, and those persons who are recognized as "third gender".

The Court gave its verdict to give fundamental rights under the Constitution to the transgender and gave directions to the state government to develop mechanisms for the civil rights of the transgender. This case made a benchmark in the domain of the rights of transgenders to select their gender identity and live life according to their choice with dignity and freedom.

In case of G. Nagalakshmi Vs. Director General of Police State of Tamil Nadu which was filed in the year 2014 in High Court of Madras set one of the example of the struggle to fight for the justice against transgender identity. Through this case, the court mandated the decision that a person has the liberty to choose their sexual or gender identity and has the right to choose their own gender.

Action Taken in terms of violating the Transgender rights:

The National Council for Transgender Persons was set up under the Transgender Persons (Protection of Rights) Act, 2019 is utilized for addressing grievances. Any atrocities done on transgender can be remedied by filing a case in the Supreme Court or High Courts under Articles 32 and 226. Anyone found violating these rights to the 'third gender' is subject to human rights abuse. The victim can appeal to the State and National Human Rights Commission.

Procedure to file complaints against discrimination of Transgender Persons

For those facing discrimination during the course of employment, either in the public or private sector, do approach the designated complaint officer set up under the Transgender Persons (Protection of Rights) Act, 2019[1].

Authorities under Transgender Law

National Council for Transgender Persons (NCTP)

On 21st August 2020, The Ministry of Social Justice and Empowerment established a National Council for Transgender Persons which constitutes a statutory body. This council governs all the policy matters that are related with the issues of transgender, intersex persons and people with diverse GIESC (Gender Identity/Expression and Sex Characteristics) identities. This council comprised of Ministry of Social Justice and Empowerment in Government, Vice-chairperson, and ex-officio;

If any parent or member of the immediate family is unable to take care of a Transgender person, the competent court shall by an order direct such person to be placed in a rehabilitation center under (Section 12(3) of the Act)

The Hindu Marriage Act (1954)

The Hindu Marriage Act or under the Special Marriage Act, 1954 mandates that a transgender person has the right to get married irrespective to any caste or religion.

The case of Arun Kumar V., Inspector General (Madras) (2019) set one of the fine examples of the law under which Transgender can get married in India. The Madras High Court declared that the marriage solemnized between a male and transgender woman to be considered as valid under the image of law.

Law for the Transgender to Protect against Sexual Harassment

The current scenario across the country observes an increase in the cases of sexual harassment at the workplace. The Government of India notified Transgender Persons (Protection of Rights) Act – Under Section 18. As per the guidelines of this Act, it is illegal for any person to sexually abuse any transgender person. This protection of Rights Act was applied in the case of Anamika V. (2020) in the High Court of Delhi. Any transgender student is eligible to file a complaint with the Internal Complaints Committee of the said school/university under this Act.

Law under the Right to Vote for Transgender

Under the Transgender Persons (Protection of Rights) Act, 2019 and The Transgender Persons (Protection of Rights) Rules, 2020, a Transgender Person who is a major (above 18 years of age) is entitled to vote in India. The voter registration form also has the option of <u>'other'</u> under the category of gender. This act gives the right to vote to the transgender person and to contest the elections as well.

Initiatives taken by the Govt. of India for Transgender Protection and Identity

The legal Law under the Transgender Persons (Protection of Rights) Act, 2019 was passed by the Parliament. The objective of this act is to access education, employment and healthcare to the transgender irrespective of gender discrimination.

Garima Greh

There is a need to safeguard the social rights of the most sensitive community of transgender. Keeping this objective in view, the `Garima Greh' scheme is established for Transgender Community. This scheme is managed and executed by the Project Management Committee (PMC) under the head of District Magistrate (DM). The aim of this scheme is to provide basic amenities, medical and recreational facilities, library facility, facilitating them to provide voter IDs, PAN card, Aadhar Card etc. To enhance the overall development of the Transgender community, this scheme provide facilities for the capacity-building and skill development programs

Pehchan

'Pehchan' was the name given to a five-year HIV program (2010-2015) that was implemented in 18 Indian states. The aim of this program is to strengthen the capacity among the MSM, transgender and Hijra communities for the improvement of HIV prevention. This program helped in building the capacity of 200 community-based organizations (CBOs) for their effective and sustainable HIV prevention.

The Global Fund support this program specifically focusing on the HIV response for vulnerable and sexual minority communities.

Conclusion

Numerous issues such as discrimination, the persistence of stigma, lack of educational facilities, unemployment, lack of home and medical facilities like HIV care and hygiene, mental stability, sexual harassment problems, forced sex work, right to property and many more are associated with the struggle for social identity of Trans-genders. Legal policies and Laws are the creations of fallible human beings and so are always subject to interpretation and criticism in terms of independent moral principles. Moreover, without the adequate implementation of legal policies and necessary social awareness, the marginalization of Trans-gender cannot be changed. Though the implementation of legal rights and laws are important for the justice of Transgender Community, however, practice of virtue of humanity is more important than providing legal policies to deal with the transgender community for their overall development in future generations.

References

- Beasley, Chris. Gender and Sexuality – Critical Theories, Critical Thinkers. New York: Sage Publications Ltd, 2005.

- Butler, J. (1990). Gender Trouble: Feminism and the Subversion of Identity. Routledge.

- Delli Swararao, K. "Hijras and their Social Life in South Asia." Imperial Journal of Interdisciplinary Research (IJIR), Vol-2, Issue – 4, 2016 pp. 515-521.

- Eckert, P., and Mc Connell, Ginet S. (2013). Language and Gender (Second ed.). New York: Cambridge University Press.

- Floyd, M., Martin, O., & Eckloff, K. J. (2019). A qualitative study of transgender individuals' experiences of healthcare including radiology. radiography, 26(2). Doi:https://doi.org/10.1016/j.radi.2019.10.008

- Michelraj, M. "Historical Evolution of Transgender Community in India" *Asian Review of Social Sciences*. ISSN: 2249-6319 Vol. 4

No. 1 (Jan-June Issue), 2015, pp. 17-19 © The Research Publication, www.trp.org.in.

• Tripathi, L. *Me Hijra, Me Laxmi.* Trans. R. Raja Rao & P.G. Joshi. New Delhi: OUP, 2015.

• Zimmerman, M. (1978-1979). Lucien Goldmann: From Dialectical Theory to Gentic Structuralism. Berkeley Journal of Sociology, 23.

Websites

• https://www.aidsdatahub.org/sites/default/files/resource/case-study-opening-spaces-transgender-communities-india.pdf.

• https://ylcube.com/c/blogs/transgender-studies-india-case-study/

• https://www.mondaq.com/india/discrimination-disability-sexualharassment/905918/transgender-rights-the-third-gender39-and-transforming-the-workplace-in-india

• https://www.mondaq.com/india/employee-rights-labour-relations/851520/analysis-transgender-persons-protection-of-the-rights-bill-2019.

• https://blog.ipleaders.in/legal-rights-of-transgender-india/

5. Legal Recognition of Transgender in India: Current Status and Challenges

Sonika Kochhar[1] and Pooja Mohobe[2]
[1]Department of Chemistry, Nagpur Institute of Technology, Nagpur
[2]Department of Chemistry, Dada Ramchand Bakhru Sindhu
Mahavidyalaya, Nagpur
Email id: drpoojamohobechemistry@gmail.com

1. Introduction

"Sex is what you are born with, gender is what you recognize and sexuality is what you discover." [Anitha Chettiar]

Section 2(k) defines a "transgender person" as an individual whose gender identity does not correspond with their biological gender. People with intersex variations, queer gender, transgender men & women, and those with certain socio-cultural identities such as kinner, hijra, aravani, jogta etc.. are included in this section.

Transgender people never have an easy time navigating the authentication of their own sexual or gender identity since they are away from established ideologies proposed about gender. Having been born with a particular sexual identity and later is realizing that their birth sex is not the true essence of who they are is very distressing stage in the life of any transgender person Transgender many a time face a great deal of violence, discrimination, and economic exclusion from society. Due to this, transgender often struggled to access basic human rights such as healthcare, education, employment and housing among others. But there are many who were able to triumph inspite of sufferings from the shackles of gender inequality that is discussed in the present paper. In order to provide protection of rights of transgender persons and their welfare, Ministry enacted the Transgender Persons (Protection of Rights) Act, (Act No. 40 of 2019) which came in to effect on 10.01.2020. The Act grants transgender people the legal status of a third gender and upholds their freedom to self-identify in accordance with their gender identity.

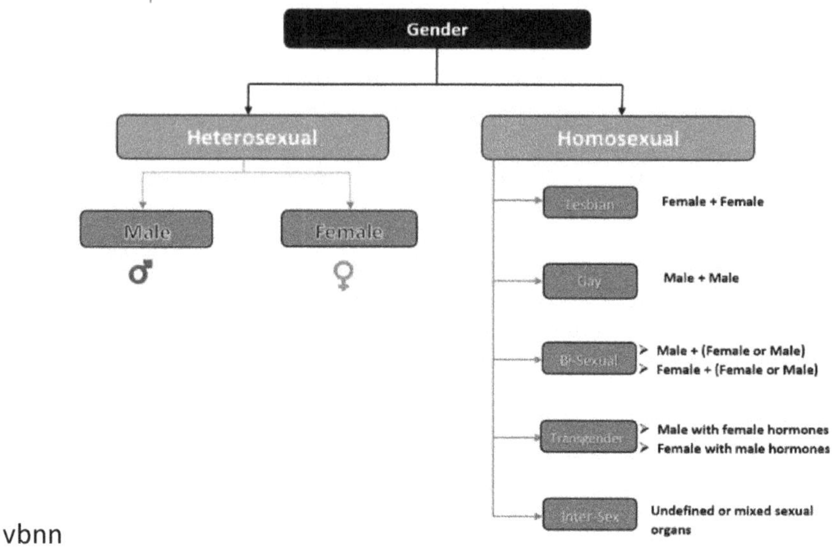

vbnn

Transgender community in India were people who did not have any identity a few decades earlier. Even their parents did not accept them. But from last few years, things began to change. Now, people stated accepting the identity and rights of transgenders. It is thus, very important to discuss this issue, understand their problems and should try to incorporate them as a part of Indian Society.

On this date, they got many rights in the Indian constitution. A major credit of it goes to a well-known transgender of India **Gauri Sawant**. Gauri was born in Mumbai in a Marathi family. His father named him Ganesh Nandan. As he grows up, he realizes about his sexuality as a Gay. However, his family did not accept this and discarded him from the family at the age of 14. He struggled a lot for his survival and fought for his identity. He then underwent vaginoplasty and defined her identity as Gauri Sawant. She stated Sakhi Char Chowghi trust in 2000 along with some of her transgender friends (Mumbai Mirror, 2017). She begins to fight for the rights of Kinner people in India. She filed a petition in the Supreme court of India in 2014 for the rights of transgenders after which Supreme Court recognized them as the third gender. Her struggle was featured in a web series "Taali" on JioCinema. Her contribution for the upliftment of transgenders is commendable.

2. Problems Faced by the Transgender Community

There are some basic problems faced by transgender in India that include exclusion from social & cultural Participation, exclusion from property, exclusion from citizen participation, lack of proper support from family, schools or colleges and society for development (Dutta and Lorway, 2019, Sinha, 2016), they face mental trauma at a young age due to continued suppression from their society which forces them to hide their true self (Ganju, & Saggurti, 2017, Chatterjee, (2018), lack of opportunities offered to gender fluidity by a gender binary led society, unavailability of true audience or readers for transgender personalities to honestly appreciate and encourage them (Mishra,& Negi ,2021).

3. Rights of the Transgender Community According to Our Constitution

3.1 Right to Equality

Article 14 of the Constitution of India, 1950 provides every person an equal status before the law and an equal protection of laws within the territory of India. The State shall not deny to any person equality before the law or the equal protection of the laws within the territory of India.

3.2 Prohibition against Discrimination

According to the Transgender Persons (Protection of Rights) Act, 2019, no person or establishment shall discriminate against a transgender person on any of the following grounds, the denial, or discontinuation of or unfair treatment in educational establishments, services, employment, occupation, healthcare services, right to reside, purchase or rent.

3.3 Right to Employment or Occupation

Supporting the objective of Article 16, the Transgender Persons (Protection of Rights) Act, (Act No. 40 of 2019) also provides that no establishment shall discriminate against any transgender person in any matter relating to employment including, but not limited to, recruitment, promotion and other related issues Article 39 (a) says that "The citizens, men and women equally have the right to adequate means of livelihood." This article should include the LGBTQ+ community to post the recognition of genders apart from men and women in cases of National Legal Services Authority. The Union of India (National Legal Services Authority, The Union of India, (2014)5 SCC 438) and Navtej Singh Jauhar, Union of India (Navtej Singh Jauhar, Union of India, (2018) 10 SCC)

3.4 Right to Life

According to Article 21 of the Constitution of India, the transgender communities have a right to a dignified life.

3.5 Right to Identity

In National Legal Services Authority v. Union of India and others (AIR 2014 SC 1863 at 1890.) the Court found that the right to self-identify one's gender, including as "third gender", was an important part of the constitutional right to live with dignity

3.6 Right to Health Care

Transgender people in India are allowed to change their legal gender post-sex reassignment surgery under legislation passed in 2019 and have a constitutional right to register themselves under a third gender.(Section 7 of the Transgender Persons (Protection of Rights) Act, (Act No. 40 of 2019) 2019)

3.7 Right to Residence

No child shall be separated from parents or immediate family on the grounds of being transgender, except on an order of a competent court, in the interest of such child. (Section 12(1) of the Transgender Persons (Protection of Rights) Act, (Act No. 40 of 2019) 2019)

3.8 Right to Education

Every educational institution funded or recognized by the appropriate Government shall provide inclusive education and opportunities for sports, recreation and leisure activities to transgender persons without discrimination on an equal basis with others. [Section 13 of the Transgender Persons Act (Protection of Rights), (Act No. 40 of 2019)]

4. Legal Recognition of Transgender Rights in India

The Transgender Persons (Protection of Rights) Act 2019

This Acts works prohibits discrimination against transgender people in the workplace, in the educational system, in the healthcare system, and in public places. The Act also makes it compulsory to establish welfare boards at the state level, whose job it will be to help these people gain access to social welfare programs. The Act also allows transgender individuals to apply for a certificate of identification, which will allow them to use a variety of services and benefits with their own gender identity. The Act also calls for the construction of distinct clinics and hospitals to offer transgender people access to proper healthcare services. In addition, the Act makes it illegal to commit crimes against transgender people, such as financial, emotional, sexual, or physical abuse. Additionally, it stipulates that those who make transgender people beg or bar them from entering public spaces like restaurants, parks, or hospitals will be held accountable. Overall, the transgender population in India has benefited greatly from the government's implementation of the Transgender Persons (Protection of Rights) Act, 2019. A more inclusive and egalitarian society is what the Act seeks to achieve by offering benefit, protection, and legal recognition to all.

Achievements and Flaws

- On September 29, 2020, the Transgender Persons Act 2020 (Protection of Rights) was implemented.

- The National Council for Transgender Persons' Constitution, which is endorsed by the transgender community and representatives of several ministries and departments

- In order to give transgender people access to basic amenities including food, medical treatment, and recreational opportunities, the ministry established 12 prototype shelter houses in nine states under the name Garima Greh: Shelter Home for Transgender People.

- The Department established a National Transgender Persons Portal, which allows any transgender person to obtain an identity card or certificate of identity without having to interact with a physical interface.

- So far, 11,000+ Certificates/ Cards issued in 32 States/UTs.

- The department through an autonomous body conducts regular awareness programs for the Community, Government Officials and various other stakeholders. More than 15,000+ participated in these programs.

- In collaboration with NITI Aayog and UNDP, the Ministry conducted five regional consultations to raise awareness of programs for the welfare of transgender people, involving all States, UTs, Civil Societies, NGOs, and the transgender community.

- Transgender Certificate of Identity can now be used as an approved supporting document while applying for Aadhar.

The Transgender Persons (Protection of Rights) Act, 2019 does not punish people who bully or harass transgender people at educational institutes or workplaces, and neither did it introduce provisions related to adoption rights, transfer of property and marriage rights of the transgenders. The act does not even provide reservation to the transgenders which would ensure their survival and also give them opportunities to progress. The act made a sexual offense against transgenders a crime but in a gender-biased way. If a cisgender woman is raped, the punishment for the rapist is imprisonment for seven years which can also extend to the death penalty whereas in the case of the rape of a trans woman, the punishment mentioned is only for 6 months which can extend by the court to a maximum of 2 years.

5. Triumph of Some Famous Transgender Personalities from India

- India only had its 1st transgender lawyer, Sathyasri Sharmila, in 2018.

- India's only transgender judge, Jyoti Mondal, in 2017.

- Prithika Yashini is the first transgender police officer from India, appointed in Tamil Nadu in 2017

- Nitasha Biswas is India's first transgender beauty pageant winner who won the Miss Trans Queen of India in 2017.

- India only had its 1st transgender police officer, K. Prithika Yashini in 2015.

- India only had its 1st transgender news anchor, actor and activist Padmini Prakashis in 2014

- India only had its 1st transgender Anjali Ameer to play a lead role in the mainstream Malayalam film industry.

- Shabnam Mausi was the first transgender from India to become a MLA from the state of Madhya Pradesh in 1998.

- Bharathi is India's first transgender pastor at the Evangelical Church of India in Chennai.

- Aryan Pasha First transgender bodybuilding champion from India.

- Sathyasri Sharmila is India's first transgender lawyer from the state of Tamil Nadu, in 2004

- Joyita Mondal became the first transgender judge from the state of Bengal. She is also credited to become the first transgender from the state to get a voter's id. Mondal also started organisations for her community like Dinajpur Notun Alo (Dinajpur New Light).

- Jiya Jas, become India's first transgender Operation Theatre Technician.

- Manabi Bandopadhyay is first transgender PhD holder and college Principal from India at Krishnagar Women's College in West Bengal. She is also an actor and her biography. She is also the person behind India's first transgender Magazine called Abomanob.

- Santa Khurai is India's first transgender to open a beauty salon in Manipur and she also led the organisation called AMANA (All Manipur Nupi Maanbi Association) which stood for creating awareness about the rights of transgender community.

- Kalki Subrahmaniam is India's first transgender Entrepreneur from the state of Tamil Nadu. She is a writer, actor, activist, journalist and founder of the organization for the transgender community called Sahodari Foundation.

- With the support from the Ministry of Social Justice and Empowerment (MSJE), a few transgender got admitted in Garima Greh, Raipur and got selected in the State Police Department of Chhattisgarh and some have been selected as Bastar fighters. Some of transgender are placed in G4S security, Vedanta group and working as security guards.

Conclusion

We live in a country that had accepted transgenders way before many other countries and our ancient texts, architecture and statues and Khajuraho statutes are proof of that. Just like the butterfly effect that is based on the analogy that if a butterfly flaps its wings in Chicago, a tornado occurs in Tokyo in short it is concluded that small actions can have great consequences. To ensure equality of all sexes we have to take little steps to achieve it. Flapping our wings might create a tornado that would destroy inequality from its root. With the three pillars of the Indian system of justice i.e. legislative, judiciary and executive, India is walking towards a better future with a positive mindset as gradually it has started recognizing the rights of the unheard through the golden doors of judicial activism. The government is also supports and provides professional vocational, training and technical institutions for the capacity building of transgender.

References

- Anitha Chettiar, "Problems Faced by Hijras (Male to Female Transgenders) in Mumbai with Reference to Their Health and Harassment by the Police" International Journal of Social Science and Humanity, Vol. 5, No. 9, September 2015, p. 752.

- Gauri Sawant – How I became a mother, Mumbai Mirror, 2018, 04(21).

- Dutta, S., Khan, S., & Lorway, R. (2019). Following the divine: an ethnographic study of structural violence among transgender jogappas in South India. Culture, Health & Sexuality: An International Journal for Research, Intervention and Care, 21(11), 1240-1256.

- Sinha, S. (2016). Social exclusion of transgender in the civil society: A case study of the status of the transgender in Kolkata. International Journal of Sociology, Social Anthropology and Social Policy, 2(1), 58-73.

- Ganju, D., & Saggurti, N. (2017). Stigma, violence and HIV vulnerability among transgender persons in sex work in Maharashtra, India. Culture, Health & Sexuality: An International Journal for Research, Intervention and Care, 19(8), 903-917.

- Chatterjee, S. (2018). Transgender shifts: Notes on resignification of gender and sexuality in India. Transgender Studies Quarterly, 5(3), 311-320.

- Mishra, U. K., & Negi, A. (2021). Transgender and the Right to Employment in India: Analysing the Trajectories of Discrimination. Bestuur, 9(1), 26-33.

6. False Representation of the Marginalized Gender by the Recent Bollywood and Tollywood

Doyel Bhattacharya, Babita Yadao, Himani Pandhurnekar, and Pooja Mohobe
Department of Chemistry
Dada Ramchand Bakhru Sindhu Mahavidyalaya, Nagpur (MS), India
Email Id: doyelnagpur@gmail.com

Introduction

With the ever-growing modernization, the influence and access of media have been increasing significantly with time. Media has the power to mould and modify public opinion (Tahir, 2012). Mass media is an influential tool to set numerous trends in the fields of arts, literature, craft. The most important trendsetter is the Bollywood. Bollywood depicts fictitious characters with an astounding sense of reality that makes an everlasting impression in the minds of the people. The most controversial of all this is the depiction of the transgender community.

The transgender community has been facing a lack of acceptance and respect over the years and subjected to harassment and violence based on their gender identity. The media portrayal of transgender as comic figures, prostitutes and violent personalities for the viewers has projected them as either victims or villains instead of their true societal representation as a human being deprived of their basic rights of equality and respect as other citizens (Gay& Lesbian Alliance Against Defamation, 2012). Media cannot act as an agent of change towards the equal depiction of transgender, but it rather illustrates them in a bizarre and nauseating manner. Most of the Bollywood movies have erroneously projected the third gender as feminine homosexual man (Jain, 2015). The songs featured on eunuchs distinctly rigorous, noisy and vulgar. Typically, in Hindi movies, hijras are always portrayed in a one-dimensional frame with no sanctity of character (Daruwalla). The reason to select the portrayal of the transgender community is that they are still facing the societal stigmatization and deprivation from their fundamental rights. Due to constant social discrimination and side facing, transgender people don't showcase their talent of being worthy and constructive for society. But this stereotypical portrayal of transgenders needs to change with time. Media can inform, educate, and entertain their viewers with objectivity, but it does not play a significant role to gain respect and right for the transgender community (Bhattacharya,2023). Shakti, a popular television soap on Colours TV, revolves around the protagonist who is transgender. People thought that Indian television underwent a revolution. It was nevertheless that late that Indian television finally chose a serious issue. The serial is about the discrimination between two sisters, Soumya and Surbhi wherein Soumya is disliked by her family members while Surbhi is the apple of their eye. However, the reason for their dislike for Soumya was revealed with time as Soumya happens to be a 'kinnar'. The fact that her mother had hidden this secret from the world and from Soumya herself is bizarre. And the worst part about it is that it is being broadcasted on television and the show is being viewed by thousands and thousands of people. This will mislead the general audience about the facts of the transgender community. The producers of the show have depicted their awareness about the present conditions of the third gender but have succumbed to the low TRPS due to low popularity. It is commendable that the makers of the serial are at least trying to talk about a serious and complicated issue. Gender overall is a complicated topic and needs to dealt with great sensitivity. As great power brings great responsibility hence television has the added responsibility of bringing about a societal reformation along with entertainment. Phirki is another Bengali TV soap of Zee Bangla that was aired from 3 February 2020- 2 January 2021. It was the first of its kind which involved the members of the transgender and LGBTQ as actors. Apart from the lead character in the serial, all other characters of trans persons were trans people themselves. The plot of the soap revolves around the societal oppression and humility that this section goes through. The serial is based on the troubled upbringing of Phirki who had been rejected by her father as she was not 'normal' like others. The trans person, Laxmi brought up Phirki as her own daughter in their community in Kolkata. The serial could not stand the pressure of low TRP and ended without any smooth or definite ending. Content analysis, thorough survey and extensive research based on personal interviews should be used as research methods. Though some attempts have been made with utmost sensitivity to bring out the gender issues, particularly in Sushmita Sen-starrer Taali. Taali has initiated a logical yet never-ending debate—Can gender be performed? While a few transgendertransexual activists and scholars strongly believe that gender is what we make of it unlike what society decides for us.

Traditionally, trans narratives were absent in mainstream cinema, with representation limited to transgender community characters appearing in song and comedy sequences. Notable songs like "Tayyab Ali Pyar ka Dushman" (Amar Akbar Anthony) and "Saj Rahi Gali Meri Maa" (Kunwara Baap) featured transgender singing and dancing. Another common practice involved male stars crossdressing, such as Rishi Kapoor in "Rafoo Chakkar," Amitabh Bachchan in "Laawaris," Aamir Khan in "Baazi," and Shah Rukh Khan in "Chamatkar." In both portrayals, the focus was on exploiting stereotypes of transgender community physicality and crossdressing for comedic effect. Furthermore, transgender were often used in significant roles, either as god-sent saviors, as seen in Rallapalli's cameo saving the protagonists' child in Mani Ratnam's "Bombay," or as wise commentators and well-wishers offering blessings. This seemed to reflect the prevailing belief in Indian society that transgenders are considered god's children, and their blessings are considered auspicious. Crude and insensitive portrayals were also present, often using an effeminate character as a comedic device making suggestive advances using sexual innuendos. These widely accepted depictions often blurred the distinctions between various sexual identities within the LGBTQ spectrum, contributing to misunderstandings (Straube, 2014). It became challenging to discern whether the character was intended to represent a transgender, intersex individual, trans person, or someone who is gay. The widespread popularity of these films perpetuated clichés and misconceptions, further exacerbating the societal lack of understanding about the lives of sexual minorities. The extravagant saris, heavy makeup, singing, dancing, and applause became enduring stereotypes associated with the transgender community. Even before these visual representations, the term 'hijra' was frequently used in cinema to signify someone as emasculated. For instance, in the movie Sholay, the famous dialogue where Kaalia asks, "Thakur ne hijron ki fauj tayyar ki hai?" exemplifies this trend. Examining the problematic portrayal of the transgender community in Bollywood prompts reflection on the impact of onscreen "trans representation" on Trans Visibility Day, especially considering Bollywood's role as a trendsetter and influential platform for social movements and artistic expression, with a massive audience of around 1.2 billion Indian viewers.

The use of cis actors to play trans roles

Recent films have chosen to explore the intricacies of transgender lives, yet there is a notable trend where cisgender actors are cast to portray transgender characters. For instance, the Sudha Kongara-directed anthology "Paava Kadhiagal" featured the film "Thangam" (2020), earning critical acclaim for its portrayal of the 27-year-old transgender Saathar, secretly in love with childhood friend Saravanan. However, the role was played by cisgender actor Kalidas Jayaram. Similarly, Vijay Sethupati's acclaimed performance in the Tamil film "Super Deluxe" (2019) faced criticism for appropriating the role of a trans woman. When media shifts its focus from artistic expression to exploiting viewers for capital gain, we witness TV series like "Patni Patni Aur Panga." Adah Sharma takes on the role of Shivani Bhatnagar in the MX Player's comedy drama, portraying a married woman in a typical newlywed couple scenario. The plot takes a turn when her husband discovers she is a transwoman, prompting him to file for divorce, citing fraud. A concerning trend in Bollywood is the consistent casting of cisgender individuals to portray trans characters. This raises questions about their ability to authentically capture the experiences of the trans community while operating within the confines of cis-heteronormativity. Movies like "Laxmii" and the recent "Chandigarh Kare Aashiqui" leave audiences pondering the filmmakers' intentions.

In "Laxmii," Akshay Kumar plays a character possessed by a female ghost who adopts "effeminate" behavior. Unfortunately, this film not only perpetuates gender stereotypes but also reinforces the misconception that transwomen are essentially men dressed in feminine attire, exhibiting effeminate behavior. The real issue lies in how transsexuality is portrayed as comedic, with the unsettling symbolism of a trans woman being depicted as an "evil ghost" terrorizing innocent people. The film fails to recognize the profound problems associated with representing trans identities in such a manner.

Similarly, with the unveiling of the "Chandigarh Kare Aashiqui" trailer, another Bollywood film attempts to raise awareness about the transgender community. In this narrative, Vaani Kapoor, portrayed as a Zumba instructor, engages in a romantic relationship with Ayushmann Khurana, a weightlifter with aspirations for national competitions. One immediate concern arises as the male lead excessively sexualizes his love interest. The film presents Vaani Kapoor as the embodiment of female beauty, prompting the male character to fall in love with her. However, the plot takes a troubling turn when Ayushmann's character discovers that his partner is a transwoman. His reaction is one of anger and accusation, claiming that he has been defrauded. This portrayal adds to the existing misconceptions surrounding transgender individuals and their relationships, failing to contribute positively to awareness efforts.

Turning trans identity into a comedy

A prevalent theme in all these films is the lack of respect for the transgender community. Despite claiming to raise awareness, they instead turn the identity of trans individuals into a source of mockery. Disturbingly, upon discovering their partner's trans identity, the characters in these films resort to misgendering, even though they had previously used correct pronouns.

Another troubling element is the notion that not coming out is akin to "tricking," "lying," or "cheating." It is problematic to base someone's identity on their outward appearance. Whether it's Shivani or Maanvi, not revealing their former gender does not constitute deception. The essence of love lies in the person, irrespective of their gender identity.

An example from "Patni Patni Aur Panga" illustrates the movie's humor reaching an unfortunate low, as the character has a nightmare depicting his wife peeing beside him in a manner stereotypically associated with cisgender men. This portrayal reflects poorly on the overall comedic quality of Bollywood films.

Conclusion

These films reinforce the harmful notion that transwomen are not authentic women but rather men who have undergone a sex change. It is crucial to advocate for movies that do not perpetuate transphobia under the guise of raising awareness. We need cinematic representations that treat trans identity with respect, acknowledging it as an integral aspect of the community rather than a secretive revelation.

Within the transgender community, there exists a subculture with its own set of norms, values, and traditions. The use of the term "farsikalaam" is an example, referring to a native language employed by members of the 'hijra' subculture. Unfortunately, this community has faced discrimination on legal, official, and social fronts, with some people wrongly perceiving them as parasites. Society, influenced by conservative beliefs, discourages interaction with 'hijras,' viewing their presence as cursed. Such unfounded fears prevent young children from engaging with them openly.

This study aims to scrutinize the portrayal of transgender individuals in Bollywood movies, seeking to understand the perspectives of transgenders regarding their representation. Additionally, the research aims to explore the experiences of transgenders concerning the role of media in raising awareness about their issues and rights.

Reviewing the literature on media representation of transgenders reveals a pattern of stereotyping, portraying them as isolated from societal norms. Many Bollywood films have consistently portrayed transgender individuals as entertainers, often pigeonholing them into comedic, thriller, or horror genres, relying on fixed visual codes like exaggerated makeup, flamboyant applause, and provocative body movements. This characterization, unfortunately, creates a sense of distance between the transgender characters and the audience. The media, particularly films, plays a pivotal role in shaping the public perception of the transgender community. To counteract fear and foster education about gender roles, media content should encourage a more accurate portrayal of transgender individuals. Television advertisements, on the other hand, often limit their depiction of transgender personalities to the context of gay and lesbian relations, contributing to a narrow and stereotypical representation. The portrayal of transgender individuals in the media tends to fall within non-representative and, in some cases, regulatory and respectful stages. Unfortunately, news related to transgender issues, whether social or legal, is often neglected or underreported by the media. Examining the impact of movies on both transgender individuals and the general public, it becomes evident that online and offline media contribute to shaping public perceptions of transgender lifestyles. Specific media messages can inadvertently perpetuate the idea that transgender identity is detrimental to society. Unconventional films, particularly those centred on the LGBT community in less cultivated regions, may lead to conflicts and negative consequences for them. Recognizing movies as a medium that reflects societal aspects and enhances understanding among viewers, it becomes essential to address the diverse recognition of the third gender in films, acknowledging the complexities it generates for the transgender community.

References

- Bhattacharya, Editor, Outlook Magazine, Gender Trouble: The Misrepresentation of Trans Identities in Indian Cinema, September 1, 2023.
- Biradar, Editor, Outlook Magazine, Lives on The Fringes: Indian Cinema's Limited Portrayal of Transgender Identity and Sexuality, September 1, 2023.
- Daruwalla, R. (n.d.). Looking at hijras through the bollywood lens. http://www.thestorypedia.com/entertainment/hijras-bollywood-lens/
- Jain, T. (2015). (Mis) representation of transgender in popular media. https://feminisminindia.com/2015/12/09/hijramedia representation/
- Panda, N. (2016). Portrayal of third gender in selected bollywood movies, 5(1). http://www.drishtithesight.com/index.php/drishti/article/view/6
- Straube, W. (2014). Trans cinema and its exit scapes. Journal of Gender Studies. http://liu.divaportal.org/smash/get/diva2:742465/FULLTEXT02.pdf
- Tahir, S. (2012). Prostitutes in Indian movies and changing perception of general public of Lahore, Pakistan: An impact study. Unpublished MS thesis. Lahore College for Women University, Lahore, Pakistan

7. Women Empowerment with Implementation of POSH Act 2013 of *"The Sexual Harassment of Women at Workplace"*

Renuka L. Roy
Seth Kesarimal Porwal College of Arts & Science & Commerce Kamptee
Email ID: royrenuka80@gmail.com
ORCID: 0000-0002-2714-160X

Introduction

In the fast-paced era of modernization and digitalization, women are at par with their male counterparts in professional as well as personal fronts. They are actively participating in academic, industrial, administrative, defence and corporate sectors with equal zeal and gusto. Yet the crime rates and news reports leave us with the impression that female professionals at organized and unorganized sectors are facing numerous incidents of sexual harassment, gender discrimination and many a times demeaning and abusive treatment at workplace. Awareness about "the Sexual Harassment of Women at Workplace" Act 2013 can really act as a tool for ensuring women empowerment. The present research paper aim at studying the secondary data recording the incidents of crime, harassments of women at workplace in organized as well as unorganized sectors in Nagpur districts. The paper will also through a slight on the salient aspects of the Act 2013 and delve on the positive results anticipated through the awareness drive organized by government about this act at workplace in the area under the purview of this study.

In the rapidly developing era of modernization and digitalization, women are working on equal footage with their male counterparts in professional as well as personal fronts. They are actively now participating in academic, industrial, administrative, defence and corporate sectors with great enthusiasm and zeal. Modernization and digitalization have brought a great change in gender roles and education plays a vital role in bringing out a shift in the outlook of the people in society. The question comes in our mind whether this modernization or digitalization is good or bad. In order to probe into the matter, it is mandatory to understand the term, "modernization".The term modernization has been defined by Britannica as, " modernization, in sociology, the transformation from a traditional, rural, agrarian society to a <u>secular</u>, urban, industrial society." (Kumar) Modern society is an industrial society, the rapid growth of industries and urbanization has brought great economic expectations from both men as well as women. Women started paving their ways in the professional world and faced numerous challenges with great metal. They tried their best to adjust and accommodate with the traditional gender role that has been perpetuated alongside their career goals. With their skills and competencies, women have carved a niche for themselves on several walks of life. They have secured for themselves equal right in decision making, equal opportunity in education, and now they have easily access to university. Society that we live is apparently liberal and modern. Yet there are some questions that are still not been properly addressed to. The issues like women's safety at workplace and equal opportunity given to women as compared to their male counterparts. The crime rates and news reports leave us with the impression that female professionals at organized and unorganized sectors are facing numerous incidents of sexual harassment, gender discrimination and many a times demeaning and abusive treatment at workplace. The atmosphere at the workplace is extremely dynamic, the intrinsic professional scenario at various strata of the society do not actually allow women to realize the fine nuances of discrimination, exploitations, and harassment that many of our sisters might be facing on an everyday basis. Their tortured psyche that had borne countless accounts of humiliation and exploitation and had scarcely attained settlement and equilibrium at the workplace.

Some of the instances of sexual harassment at the workplace in India need to be thoughtfully considered. Aruna Ramchandra Shanbaug who was born on 1st June, 1948 was a nurse by profession at <u>King Edward Memorial Hospital</u>, <u>Parel</u>, <u>Mumbai</u>. Her case was one of the prime court cases, which was also famous for the unprecedented nature of crime and victim. On 24th January, 2011, Shanbaug was brutally raped by a ward boy, Sohanlal Bhartha Walmiki. Followed by this incident, owing to some severe injuries Shambaug went into coma and remained in a vegetative state for nearly 37 years. Pinki Virani, a philanthropist journalist filed a plea for euthanasia to the Supreme Court. After a rigorous medical examination, the court rejected the petition on 7 March 2011. Unfortunately, Shanbaug died on 18th May, 2015 due to pneumonia. The case reached its fame due to the never before request of mercy killing of the patient in the vegetative stage, but no one thought of the sufferings of Aruna owing to the heinous act of sexual assault and abuse by her male colleague. Eventually, in its landmark decision, the Indian Supreme legalized passive euthanasia in year 2018.

The status of any society is determined by the way it treats its most vulnerable sections like women, children, and old people. As a civilized citizen, it is our paramount duty to safeguard their rights and prevent them from any untoward circumstances. Women at workplaces are exposed to high level of risks due to the threat of sexual assault in their place of work. There felt a need of a robust mechanism to combat the menacing situation at workplace, so that women get a free and secure work atmosphere. The verdict given by the honorable judges of the Supreme Court in Vishaka case was a milestone judgment in working women's long crusade for justice. This decision proved to be an important guideline to combat the problem of sexual harassment of women at workplaces. The verdict was given by a three-judge bench comprising of Chief Justice Verma, Justice Sujata V. Manohar and Justice B.N. Kripal. The government of India brought the Sexual Harassment of Women at Workplace (Prevention, Prohibition, Redressal) Act 2013 on 22nd April, 2022. The provisions made in the act were supporting the dignified existence of working women in organized as well as unorganized sectors.

An Act to provide protection against sexual harassment of women at workplace and for the prevention and redressal of complaints of sexual harassment and for matters connected therewith or incidental thereto. WHEREAS sexual harassment results in violation of the fundamental rights of a woman to equality under articles 14 and 15 of the Constitution of India and her right to life and to live with dignity under article 21 of the Constitution and right to practice any profession or to carry on any occupation, trade or business with includes a right to a safe environment free from sexual harassment; AND WHEREAS the protection against sexual harassment and the right to work with dignity are universally recognized human rights by international conventions and instruments such as Convention on the Elimination of all Forms of Discrimination against Women, which has been ratified on the 25th June 1993 by the Government of India; AND WHEREAS it is expedient to make provisions for giving effect to the said Convention for protection of women against sexual harassment at workplace. (THE SEXUAL HARASSMENT OF WOMEN AT WORKPLACE)

The Government of India constituted an Internal Complaints Committee in order to implement this act in all the organized and unorganized sectors and set the monitoring bodies like the Ministry of Women and Children Development and Mahila Ayog etc. The Ministry of Women and Children Development, the Government of India has launched an online complaint management system called SHE- -Box. Once a complaint is submitted to, She-Box, it will be directly sent to the Internal Complaint Committee (ICC) of the concerned Ministry/ Department/ PSU/ Autonomous Body etc. having jurisdiction to inquire into the complaint. It becomes easier for the complainant as well as the nodal administrative authority to keep an eye on the progress of inquiry by the Internal Complaints Committee of the concerned ministry. The National Commission for Women constitute the several committees to monitor the cases of sexual harassment of women at workplace coming from all the corners of India and take due cognizance in terms of addressing the issues and in meeting out justice.

Nagpur District is committed to provide all professional women working for organized and unorganized sectors that fall within its jurisdiction a safe and healthy place of work and study, free from abusive and menacing treatment and sexual exploitation in the form of undue favours of any kind at the workplace. As per the guidelines from the Women and Children Development, the National Commission for Women, the Supreme Court, the institute has established an Internal Complaint Committee (ICC) for effective enforcement of gender equality and assurance of an environment free of sexual harassment founded on fundamental human rights and to abstain from abuse of any kind. According to the Sexual Harassment of Women at Workplace (Prevention, Prohibition and Redressal) Act, 2013, sexual harassment includes undesirable sexually determined actions including:

- Physical contact and advances

- A demand or request for sexual favours

- Sexually coloured remarks

- Showing pornography

- Any other unwelcome physical, verbal or non-verbal conduct of sexual nature.

Harassing a woman at the workplace is a clear violation of her right to work as an equal and liberated individual at the workplace. The lewd approaches of male colleagues at workplaces surely create an atmosphere of insecurity and hostility for female folks. Eventually, many of them opt to drop out and settle at home. The non-participation of half of our intellectual, sincere and hardworking population leads to adverse effects of women's economic empowerment and the nation's goal of inclusive growth.

As Former Mayor of Nagpur has rightly pointed out Nanda Jichkar has rightly pointed out "Watching members of Maharashtra State Commission for Women (MSCW) tirelessly makes me wonder how well women can be empowered if we think as a human-being." (Support women in government offices, mayor tells male employ ..) In Nagpur District several workshops are held at various public places, administrative bodies, government offices, schools, and colleges etc. During these sensitization activities generating awareness about harassment of women at workplace, gender discrimination, exploitation etc. are brought into focus. Forums like PUSH (People United against Sexual Harassment) have done yeoman's service in changing the mindset of the people. The training sessions are organized in the Nagpur district focused on orienting the employees about the modalities of the Internal Complaints Committee and the methodology employed to redress the complaints in such cases. During the sensitization workshops, the women are encouraged to speak out and lodge a complaint rather than suppressing their voices with a sense of guilt or dishonour.

References

1. "Aruna Shanbaug case." n.d. *Wikipedia.* 26 12 2022. https://en.wikipedia.org/wiki/Aruna_Shanbaug_case

2. Kumar, Krishna. "Modernization." 5 December 2022. *Britannica.* 26 12 2022. https://www.britannica.com/topic/modernization

3. "Support women in government offices, mayor tells male employ .." 12 July 2017. *Times of India.* Online. 26 12 2022.

https://timesofindia.indiatimes.com/city/nagpur/support-women-in-govt-offices-mayor-tells-male employees/articleshow/59552216.cms

4. "The Sexual Harassment Of Women At Workplace." 22nd April 2013. online. 26 12 2022. https://legislative.gov.in/sites/default/files/A2013-14.pdf

8. The Fight Against Marital Abuse as Depicted in the Hollywood Movie *Provoked*

Suman Keswani
Department of Languages
Dada Ramchand Bakhru Sindhu Mahavidyalaya, Nagpur
Email ID: suman.keswani2018@gmail.com

Introduction

The victimization of women in the name of marriage is still common in all strata of society. Even today in the Indian patriarchal system, women are subjected to beatings, insults, physical abuse, slavery, and marital rape by their abusive husbands. The reasons may vary from anger issues, ego hassles, demand of dowry, or severe personality disorders. Though the same may happen to men also, the ratio as evident from statistics reveals that women are the victims of domestic violence and marital abuse to a larger extent.

A thought-provoking Hollywood film *Provoked* an adaptation of the book *Circle of Light* deals with the same theme and gives a clear picture that battered women may take some extreme steps like even murdering their husbands but the law has to empathize with these women because of their mental state tends to diminish as they have been subjected to utmost cruelty for years at the hands of their husbands. The law needs to rethink the proper meaning of the word 'provoked' or 'unprovoked' by trying to understand the case fully from the battered woman's perspective. According to the Cambridge dictionary the meaning of the word 'provoked' is try "to make a person or an animal angry or annoyed".

(https://dictionary.cambridge.org/dictionary/english/provoke).

The Book *Circle of Light*

The book *Circle of Light, the Autobiography of Kiranjit Ahluwalia* was written by Rahila Gupta and Kiranjit Ahluwalia (Gupta, Rahila 1997). It was originally published by Harper Collins, and in 388 pages depicted the story of a helpless woman Kiranjit caught in a turbulent marriage.

This book has been adapted into a Hollywood film *Provoked* by Eros International and Mauj Telecom Partner.

The Film *Provoked*

The Hollywood film *Provoked* is directed by Jag Mundhra and produced by Sunanda Murali Manohar

(https://youtu.be/nDozwK08uNE?si=kcbyq1djjURBRPA4).

Apt screenplay by Rahila Gupta and Carl Austin lends a realistic depiction of the life and agonies of Kiranjit whose role is enacted convincingly by the beautiful actress Aishwarya Rai. She brings the much-evident innocence to the character and her expressive eyes bring out the emotion, fear, confusion, and moral dilemma ingrained in her personality because of her traditional upbringing. Nandita Das shines in her role of social activist Radha who fights for women's rights. The film depicts the agony of females trapped in abusive marriages. Actors Aishwarya Rai Bachchan, Naveen Andrew, Miranda Richardson, Rebecca Pidgeon, and Nandita Das have put forward splendid performances to lend a realistic look to the well-presented story. The themes of female subjugation, marital abuse, and battered women syndrome have been dealt with in the autobiography and the movie adaptation as well. The film shows at length the severe torture against Ms. Kiran Ahluwalia at the hands of her husband Deepak. It is based on the true story of Kiran, a Punjabi woman who has been a victim of marital abuse for ten years. She is convicted of murdering her husband in a fit of anger. The final transformation of Kiranjit and her revolt against the injustice meted out on her, form the crux of the movie. The title of the movie 'Provoked' is significant and plays a pivotal role in shaping the plot, as the legal proceedings of the murder case rest on the clear understanding of the word 'provoked'.

Plot of the Film

Kiranjit was born and brought up in Punjab State of India. She lost her father at a tender age and her mother died of cancer when she was sixteen years old. She was the youngest of nine children and was married off to Deepak in a haste. She shifted to London with him and began her new life. She tried a lot to please her husband but Deepak was an insecure, jealous, hypocrit type of person. He put inhuman restrictions on Kiranjit and started beating and abusing her within days of their marriage. During a heated altercation, he pushed Kiran, then in an advanced pregnancy stage, down the stairs. He even tried to burn her face with a hot iron. Under alcohol intoxication, he used to rape her every night. After bearing repeated beatings and insults Kiranjit decided to teach him a lesson and to give him some pain too which she had to bear. One night in May 1989 she emptied a petrol can on the bed while Deepak was sleeping and set him on fire. Deepak jumped off the bed and fled down the stairs. Kiranjit was arrested as Deepak blamed her for trying to kill him. Kiranjit accepted her crime and she was placed in Mullwood Hall Jail. Later Deepak succumbed to his injuries. Kiranjit was sentenced to 12 years of rigorous imprisonment for the murder of her husband. Police constable James Connell testified that Kiranjit was alert and completely in her senses when he first saw her just after the incident. This testimony was actually as per the instructions of his senior who had told him to say so.

The highlight of the movie are the scenes related to the two court trials, the first one- the initial hearing and the second one- the appeal for the second hearing. Most of the scenes are filmed in Mullwood Hall prison where Kiranjit was kept as a prisoner. The bond she shares with her fellow prisoner Ronnie (played by Miranda Johnson) adds an emotional flavor to the film. In comparison to her ten years of living with her husband, she felt free in jail. But as prevalent in battered women's syndrome, she had horrible dreams of her earlier life when she was abused and raped daily by her husband. In jail she was supported by her new friends and she regained her self-confidence slowly. The fight against hooliganism in jail, Ronnie's suicide attempt, and Kiranjit saving Ronnie at the nick of the moment, the power of staying united from all these experiences she became stronger.

Plot Development

With the cooperation from her jail mates, Kiranjit was able to come out of the mental trauma and decided to fight for her rights. Radha, the social activist played by fine actor Nandita Das finally became a savior for Kiranjit. She convinced Kiranjit that she would get justice but she would have to write down her life story for people to read and feel her pain. Radha, Anil Gupta the lawyer, Ronnie the friend, Lord Foster (Ronnie's brother and the Queen's Counsel) as well as the repentant Police Constable James Connell managed to fight for Kiranjit and appeal to the High Court questioning the earlier verdict. It was

Radha who being a woman, could empathize with Kiranjit that since ten years Kiran had been bearing physical, and mental abuse silently, then one night she could not bear it anymore and the volcano just erupted and she killed her husband. She could understand this and asked her friends, was this so difficult to understand? She stated further that the judge didn't tell Kiranjit's story to the jury which would have proved her to be a distressed woman.

Court Trial

The court scenes where Lord Foster presented his three submissions to the court are undoubtedly the best scenes that turned the table and provided a ray of hope for Kiranjit. Lord Foster claimed that the initial verdict delivered on 7th December 1989 was wrong and he gave three important submissions for the same. He challenged the word 'provoked' and declared that the interpretation of 'provocation' given by the Honorable Judge to the jury was erroneous. He used an example of the Regina vs Daffy case and said that comparing Kiranjit's case with Regina one was a mistake. He went on to elaborate on the true meaning of the word 'provocation' in his first submission.

The judge had claimed during the initial hearing that there was a time period of two hours which is the cooling off period between the act of cruelty by the husband and the crime for which Kiranjit was punished, which should not be considered as provocation. Foster argued that for a woman who was a victim of beatings and insults for ten years and who also feared for her life and for her children's life too, considering this two hours cooling period was not enough for such a battered woman. He clearly read out the Homicide act of 1959- "Where there is evidence on which the jury can find that the defendant was provoked to lose his self-control, the question of whether it was enough to make a reasonable person do as they did, shall be left to the jury."

(https://youtu.be/nDozwKO8uNE?si=kcbyq1djjURBRPA4)

During the court trial the lawyer gave the second submission that the mental state of the victim was not understood by the jury. Lord Foster went on to elaborate the meaning of "battered women's syndrome" wherein because of continued persecution, the personality of the victims is altered and they go into a state of learned helplessness, a term well-known by psychiatrists. He blasted out that the jury should have been clearly told about Kiranjit's chaotic life and struggles, and after that the decision should have been finalized about her punishment.

Discussion

The film *Provoked* about distressed women and their rights sent strong messages across all the existing societies that had adhered to male dominance and patriarchal systems. The lawyer managed to raise some serious questions related to the punishments to distressed women. The final submission by the lawyer on the grounds of 'diminished responsibility' proved to be the game-changer. Lord Foster presented Police Constable James Connell's revised statement that the accused, when he saw her first, was not alert nor was she in her senses. She was totally oblivious of her surroundings and seemed to be in trauma. Also the psychiatrist's report affirmed the Constable's statement. The psychiatrist had mentioned that just after the incident and before the hearing the accused's mental state had reduced. Lord foster pleaded with the court that Kiranjit had witnessed two big injustices in her life, one from her abusive husband and the other from the court through the wrong verdict. To correct the initial doings was impossible but by accepting her appeal at least they could correct the second injustice. After hearing the lawyer's argument, the judge came to the conclusion that it was a mistake on the part of the court to overlook that the accused was in a mental state called 'endogenous depression' just after the incident as mentioned by the psychiatrist. So he gave permission for a second hearing. Finally, after three years and four months of her imprisonment, the sentence was changed from murder to manslaughter and as a justification to the time already spent in jail Kiranjit Ahluwalia was released.

Message of the Film

The message of the fight against injustice and revolt for rights is delivered strongly in the movie. The final scene where Kiranjit speaks out her heart that life is not for bearing crimes silently brings tears into the eyes of the audience. She further states that it is every mother's duty to teach her sons to love and respect women's pride. This scene is heart-wrenching and makes the audience introspect whether they are imparting such values to their children or not. At the end of the movie it is mentioned that in 2001 Kiranjit Ahluwalia was honored by Prime Minister Tony Blair's wife Cherie Booth with the "Asian Woman Role

Model Award " for her courage and grit. The title of the movie- the word 'provoked' is apt as the whole movie rests on the true meaning of that word and its relevance in the case. Also at the end it is displayed on the screen that -

"Regina vs Ahluwalia became the monumental court case that changed the nature of British law forever, as affords the "Provocation Defense"- the acceptance of Battered Women Syndrome as a legal state of mind, in accordance with defendants who have suffered extended physical abuse at the hands of a spouse.

Conclusion

Marital abuse should not be tolerated in society. In this era of gender equality, it is shameful that even today women are not safe, not in streets, nor in their own homes. Stringent laws are needed for women's safety so that they can be saved from disrespect, abuse and other crimes, then only true progress can be attained. In crimes related to women or committed by women, an extra sensitive approach on the grounds of empathy should be followed because women try to remain silent about their sufferings on account of shame and backlash from the orthodox society. Fast-track courts should be set up for speedy trials of cases.The Hollywood film *Provoked* proved to be an eye-opening film that educated the masses about women's rights.

References

- Gupta,Rahila.*Circle of Light: An Autobiography* https:/books.google.co.in 1997

- Provoked https://youtu.be/nDozwKO8uNE?si=kcbyq1djjURBRPA4)

- https://g.co/kgs/zeqrMTd)

- https://dictionary.cambridge.org/dictionary/english/provoke

9. Transgender and Women's Empowerment in India: A Historical and Cultural Perspective

S. Bhagchandani 'Aashna'[1] and Damini Motwani[2]
[1]Department of Biotechnology
[2]Department of Biochemistry
Dada Ramchand Bakhru Sindhu Mahavidyalaya, Nagpur
Email ID: sharda.spforever@gmail.com

Introduction

India, a land of diverse cultures, has a rich and complex history regarding gender and identity. The roles and rights of women and transgender individuals have evolved significantly over time. This chapter explores the historical context, cultural nuances, and current scenarios of transgender and women's empowerment in India, highlighting the struggles, achievements, and ongoing challenges faced by these communities.

Historical Context

Transgender Individuals in Ancient and Medieval India

Transgender individuals, often referred to as hijras, have a long history in India. Ancient texts like the Mahabharata and Ramayana mention characters with fluid gender identities. For instance, Shikhandi in the Mahabharata is depicted as a warrior who changes gender, and Aravan, the son of Arjuna, is married to a transgender woman.

In medieval India, hijras held significant social roles. They were often employed in royal courts as advisors, performers, and guardians of harems. The Mughal era, in particular, saw hijras enjoying certain privileges and recognition, though their societal status fluctuated with changing political landscapes.

Women's Roles in Historical India

Women's status in ancient India varied considerably across different regions and periods. Vedic literature suggests that women enjoyed considerable respect and educational opportunities. However, later periods saw a decline in their status due to social practices like Sati, child marriage, and purdah (seclusion). Reform movements in the 19th and 20th centuries, led by figures like Raja Ram Mohan Roy and Mahatma Gandhi, played a crucial role in challenging these oppressive customs and advocating for women's rights.

Cultural Perspective

Transgender Identity in Indian Culture

Transgender identities in India are not merely a contemporary concept but are deeply rooted in the cultural fabric. The hijra community is often associated with blessings and rituals, particularly during childbirth and marriage, reflecting a unique blend of reverence and marginalization. Despite their ritual importance, hijras have historically faced social ostracization and economic hardships.

Culturally, the hijra identity is distinct from the Western notion of transgender. It encompasses a complex mix of gender fluidity, community bonds, and spiritual roles. This unique cultural position has influenced the way transgender rights are viewed and advocated for in modern India.

Women in Indian Culture

Indian culture traditionally places women in roles tied to family and domestic responsibilities. However, this has been evolving, especially in urban areas. Women are now increasingly participating in education, the workforce, politics, and leadership positions. Cultural festivals like Durga Puja and Navratri celebrate feminine power, symbolizing strength and resilience.

Legal and Social Reforms

Legal Milestones for Transgender Rights

The legal recognition of transgender rights in India has seen significant progress in recent years. The landmark 2014 Supreme Court judgment in NALSA v. Union of India legally recognized transgender individuals as a third gender, granting them the right to self-identify their gender. This ruling mandated the government to provide reservations in education and employment and ensure access to healthcare and other essential services.

In 2019, the Transgender Persons (Protection of Rights) Act was enacted, aiming to protect transgender individuals from discrimination in employment, education, and healthcare. However, the Act has faced criticism from activists for not adequately addressing issues like self-identification and the involvement of medical boards in gender recognition processes.

Women's Empowerment Initiatives

Women's empowerment in India has been bolstered by numerous legal and policy measures. The enactment of laws like the Dowry Prohibition Act, Protection of Women from Domestic Violence Act, and amendments to the Hindu Succession Act to ensure equal inheritance rights have been pivotal.

The government has also launched various schemes like Beti Bachao Beti Padhao (Save the Daughter, Educate the Daughter), which aims to improve the status of girls in society through education and financial incentives. Women's representation in politics has seen a boost through reservations in local governance bodies, ensuring a significant presence of women in decision-making processes.

Current Scenario

Transgender Empowerment Today

Despite legal advancements, transgender individuals in India continue to face significant challenges. Social acceptance remains low, and discrimination in employment, healthcare, and housing is rampant. However, there are signs of progress. Increased visibility in media and politics, along with grassroots activism, has started to shift public perceptions.

Organizations like the Humsafar Trust and the Naz Foundation work tirelessly to support transgender individuals through healthcare services, legal aid, and advocacy. The election of transgender individuals to political positions, like Shabnam Mausi in Madhya Pradesh and Gauri Sawant in Maharashtra, marks a significant step towards greater inclusion.

Women's Empowerment Today

Women's empowerment in contemporary India is marked by significant strides and persistent challenges. Women are making their mark in various fields, from business and technology to sports and politics. High-profile examples include the success of women in the Indian Space Research Organisation (ISRO) and the rise of female entrepreneurs like Kiran Mazumdar-Shaw.

Despite these achievements, gender inequality remains pervasive. Issues like gender-based violence, pay disparity, and underrepresentation in certain sectors continue to hinder progress. Nevertheless, the rise of feminist movements and increased awareness through media and education are fostering a more inclusive environment for women's empowerment.

Conclusion

The journey of transgender and women's empowerment in India is a testament to the resilience and determination of these communities. While significant progress has been made through legal reforms and cultural shifts, much work remains to be done. Continued advocacy, inclusive policies, and societal change are essential to ensure that transgender individuals and women can fully realize their rights and potential in a more equitable India.

By understanding the historical and cultural contexts, we can better appreciate the complexities and nuances of gender empowerment in India, paving the way for a future where all individuals, regardless of gender, can thrive.

The references used in this chapter provides a robust foundation for understanding the historical, cultural, and current perspectives on transgender and women's empowerment in India. They cover scholarly articles, legal documents, and reports from relevant organizations, ensuring a comprehensive and well-rounded chapter.

References

1. Historical Context of Transgender Individuals

- Sharma, A. (2000). "Transgender in India: Understanding Hijras and Aravanis." Journal of Indian Studies, 7(2), 85-103.
- Reddy, G. (2005). With Respect to Sex: Negotiating Hijra Identity in South India. University of Chicago Press.

2. Women's Roles in Historical India

- Chakravarti, U. (1993). "Conceptualising Brahmanical Patriarchy in Early India: Gender, Caste, Class and State." Economic and Political Weekly, 28(14), 579-585.
- Thapar, R. (1975). A History of India: Volume One. Penguin Books.

3. Cultural Perspective of Transgender Identity

- Nanda, S. (1999). Neither Man nor Woman: The Hijras of India. Wadsworth Publishing.
- Hossain, A. (2012). "The Paradox of Recognition: Hijra, Third Gender and Sexual Rights in India." Culture, Health & Sexuality, 14(9), 1041-1055.

4. Women in Indian Culture

- Kumar, R. (1993). The History of Doing: An Illustrated Account of Movements for Women's Rights and Feminism in India, 1800-1990*. Zubaan.
- Sharma, K. (2007). "Gender Roles in India." Journal of South Asian Studies, 30(1), 123-134.

5. Legal Milestones for Transgender Rights

- Supreme Court of India. (2014). National Legal Services Authority vs. Union of India.
- Ministry of Social Justice and Empowerment. (2019). The Transgender Persons (Protection of Rights) Act.

6. Women's Empowerment Initiatives

- Government of India. (2005). Protection of Women from Domestic Violence Act.
- Government of India. (2015). Beti Bachao Beti Padhao Yojana.

7. Current Scenario of Transgender Empowerment

- Narrain, A., & Bhan, G. (2005). Because I Have a Voice: Queer Politics in India. Yoda Press.
- Humsafar Trust. (2021). "Annual Report on Transgender Rights and Advocacy in India." Humsafar Trust Publications.

8. Current Scenario of Women's Empowerment

- Tandon, N. (2016). "Women in Science and Technology: A Case Study of ISRO." Journal of Science and Technology Policy Management, 7(3), 215-230.
- Rao, N. (2018). "Entrepreneurial Women in India: The Case of Kiran Mazumdar-Shaw." Women's Studies International Forum, 68, 127-135.

10. Women, Caste and Reform

Anshu Choudhary
Department of English
DRB Sindhu Mahavidyalaya, Nagpur
Email ID: anshuchoudhary0612@gmail.com

Introduction

Although the seeds of social reformation were sown in the ancient Indian soils comprising of Vedic age they began to germinate slowly. The first major social reformation that happened in Indian society was in early 19th century, when for the first time Raja Ram Mohan Roy raised his voice against ' Sati Pratha ', " the act or custom of a Hindu widow burning herself to death or being burned to death on the funeral pyre of her husband." This magnum opus reform gave way too many other social reformations like child marriage, infanticide, widow remarriage, eradication of the caste system and most importantly emancipation and education for women for enlightenment and progress in society. Social reformers are people who are common and want to bring change in society in an extraordinary way.

Raja Ram Mohan Roy was the founder of one of the first Indian socio-religious reform movements of Brahmo Samaj. A great scholar, an independent, religious and social reformer popularly known as the "father of modern India" and fondly given the title" Raja " he devoted his life for religious, social and political reforms.His fight against " Sati Pratha " paved the way to many other reformations in Indian society. He was the man who fought against orthodoxies and superstitions.He was the pioneer in Indian education and the trendsetter whose ideologies became an example for many other social reformers of the time like Ishwar Chand Vidyasagar, Swami Vivekananda, Swami Dayanand Saraswati, Mahatma Jyotiba Phule, Srimati Savitri Bai Phule, Bhimrao Ambedkar, Mahatma Gandhi, Baba Amte, Vinoba Bhave, Mother Teressa and many others.

Swami Vivekananda was also one of the renowned social reformers of India. Vivekananda's main goal was to remove the weakness in Indian society, both physically and mentally. He didn't initiate any social change,but through his speeches and writings, he gave a message against social and religious evils. He was against religious belief and superstition & in his speeches, he used to claim enthusiastically against social evils & became one of the important social reformers in India. He inspired the minds of the youth of the country. He believed that women could change India. He stood against all kinds of religious, intellectual and social evils issued by the orthodox and believed that untouchability should be eliminated if the nation wants to progress. His speeches inspired the national development for freedom and his life is still a source of motivation for the nation.

Swami Dayanand Saraswati was one of the well-known social reformers of India. Swami Dayanand Saraswati was in favour of teaching Vedas hence he gave a slogan: 'Return of the Vedas '. He was against all the wrong things going on in the name of Hinduism and tried to promote Hindu philosophy again. He aggressively opposed to all social evils like caste system, he was a supporter and advocate of women's right to education and equal social status, as well as he campaigned against untouchability and child marriage. He was a supporter of community marriage and widow marriage, as well as fought for the freedom of the Shudras. He also encouraged women to read the Vedas. He was a founder Of the Arya Samaj. His main goal was to reform Hindu religion, to re-establish Vedic religions in true form, uniting India socially, religiously and politically and preventing the Western influence on Indian civilizations and culture. According to Annie Besant Dayanand Saraswati was the person who acknowledged that "India is for Indians ".

Ishwar Chandra Vidyasagar was social reformer in the 19th century. Amongst all the reformers Vidyasagar was a very strong social reformer, who was not afraid to fight against any social injustice. Their main contribution was in raising the status of women. These widows were great supporters of marriage. Among Hindus, the condition of women in those days was not as good as today. Vidyasagar worked very hard continuously for the betterment of women. For this he proposed making of laws for widow remarriage. He also raised his voice against polygamy and child marriage. Vidyasagar's contribution to the field of education is incompatible. The change that was initiated by Raja Ram Mohan Roy was continued by him he also was aware of the activities of the Brahmo Samaj.

Mahatma Jyotiba Phule was also a famous social reformer in India. He was the first who initiated the most important work which was the education of women. In 1848 Jyotiba opened the first school in the country for girls, to create an equal society. Though he had social pressure and threats, he did not diverge from his goal and continued to fight against social evils and spread awareness among people against it. Jyotiba Phule went against the social practice of child marriage against the child marriage and an enthusiast for widow re-marriage. The name 'Dalit' was coined by him for the first time for untouchables, who were broken, disturbed and exploited. To uplift the lower castes and untouchables, on 24th Sept 1873, he founded a society named, the Satyashodhak sSamaj. The main objective of this society was that no one should be discriminated against on the basis of caste, religion and gender and an equal society should be created. Satyashodhak Samaj was also against religious practices and superstitions like idolatry, priests as a middleman between men and god in religious rituals and ceremonies etc.

Babasaheb Ambedkar was also one of the well-known social reformers of India. The main objective of Dr Ambedkar was to fight for the rights of the lower castes and the untouchables and to root out from the evil. He demanded the reservation for such communities. He initiated the benefit of reservation for Scheduled Castes (SC) and Scheduled Tribes (ST) in the Constitution of India in 1950. As Ambedkar was the chairman of the drafting committee, he had contributed immensely in creating a modern India. This constitution had the most important aspect which was to bring equality in the social, political and economic condition of the untouchables. He felt that they are emphatically women and scheduled castes and scheduled tribes and OBCs; therefore, special provisions were added for their rise. The discriminations that were faced by them were eliminated.

Acharya Vinoba Bhave has played a vital role as a humanist and social reformer of India. His main contribution was in the Bhumi-dan movement which started from Pochampally in Telangana. Gradually this movement gained momentum and has roamed all over India and asked the landlords to give land to the poor farmers. After receiving the land as a gift, it was given to the poor people to cultivate. Hence, through his Bhoodan movement he tried to provide social justice to the people. To make women independent and self-sufficient he accustomed an ashram and community in food production. He was also a believer of religious generosity and tried to convince the common people in his writing and teaching. He was very impressed with the Gita and translated it into the Marathi language. He also translated many religious writings such as the Gita, Quran and Bible. Throughout his life, he continued to follow Mahatma Gandhi's principles and served society.

Baba Amte was yet another well-known social reformer of modern India. For him Mahatma Gandhi was an exemplar, he followed his principles and the way of living his life. His contribution for India and its society was significantly be seen in the form of service, rehabilitation and empowering the people who were suffering from leprosy (A chronic, curable infectious disease mainly causing skin lesions and nerve damage). In addition, Baba Amte also brought awareness amongst people about importance of trees and forest, the ecological balance and wildlife conservation. He fought for the rights and had also joined the Narmada Bachao Andolan.

Mother Teresa was the most famous social reformer of India. She devoted her entire life for the needy and poor people in the society. It was her efforts, that people from different religions and castes together contributed for the needy and poor people of India. Low caste and untouchable people who were not touched by doctors and physicians and also not served by their own people, died due to lack of medicine. After seeing the situation of the poor people in the city, she decided to open a school and build a shelter house for those left by the family for fear of infectious diseases. She served all those who were poor, weaker section and who all were dying. Mother Teresa and her organization used to go out on the streets and pick up people whose families had abandoned them. Mother Teresa built 20 missionary homes for the children living on the streets, these missionaries were the only shelter for them.

Medha Patkar is a well-known social reformer of India. She is known all over the world as the 'voice of the Narmada Valley'. She fought for the rights of the people especially for those, 37 thousand villages affected by the 'Sardar Sarovar Project'. She also led the movement of displaced Maheshwar Dam. Writers like Arundhati Roy have been her close associates. She taught the students how to work in the field of social science. Her organization has done a lot of work to improve basic education, health and drinking water conditions. She is also credited for connecting all the reformation movements in India with each other. She started a network called National Alliance for People's Movement. The mass movement in the country was redefined by Medha Patkar, one of the leading social worker of our country.

Conclusion

Thus, in the light of foregoing discussion over position of women, caste and reforms we find that like male reformers, women reformers have also contributed a lot for the recognition and growth of Indian society. There is a long aesthetic and experiential journey of feminine sensibility in bringing up change in the society. Efforts by women reformers are also worth reading, full of energy and enthusiasm. Women have well contributed to the social consciousness in the society, caught in the male storm of historical conflicts and turmoil and change. They have raised the problems of cultural identity and also written at length about of traditional values in relation to changing realities, both in our society and in our collective personality. I feel, the contribution of women is immense in terms of expressing her thoughts through her actions as a reformer, even culturally she can bring change in the society, her identity as a women marks a difference . Social consciousness, unique themes and arresting techniques, reflection of socio-political concerns, and contemplation over moral, spiritual and mystical aspects of life are the genres where women can definitely bring changes which will help in rebuilding the society

References

- Naik, M .K.(1982): A History of Indian English Literature. New Delhi :Sahitya Academi
- Prasad, H.M. & Singh C.P. (Ed.).(1985): Indian Poetry in English, Sterling Publishing pvt. Ltd.
- Dwivedi, A. N.(1984, reprint 2008): Studies in Contemporary Indo-English Verse, Vol.1.
- Tilak, Raghukul (2011): New Indian English Poets and Poetry, Rama Brothers India Ltd., New Delhi.
- https://www.boloji.com/articles/49813/contemporary-indian-english-poetry
- https://feminisminindia.com/2017/07/24/meena-kandasamy-ms-militancy
- https://magadhuniversity.ac.in/download/econtent/pdf/Religio us%20and%20Social%20Reform%20of%20India-converted.pdf

- https://www.indiacelebrating.com/general-awareness/social-reformers-of-india
- https://www.ritiriwaz.com/social-reforms-in-india/#:~:text=Social%20reforms%20became%20an%20integral%20part%20of%20religious,reforms%20movements%20have%2%200aimed%20at%20uprooting%20social%20evils.
- https://www.yourarticlelibrary.com/history/social-reforms-made-by-raja-ram-mohan-roy-2/47606.
- https://www.ukessays.com/essays/english-literature/the-representation-of-marginalised-voices-in-poetry-english-literature-essay.php
- https://www.goodreads.com/shelf/show/marginalized-voices

11. Unheard Voices of the Relegated Mythological Female Characters

Hritika L Hisaria
PGT English
Sunflag School, Bhandara
Email ID: hritikahritika30@gmail.com

Introduction

Indian mythology is a treasure trove of captivating stories and larger-than-life characters and among these, women play pivotal roles that are both inspiring and thought-provoking.

These mythical women exhibit a wide range of qualities and characteristics, transcending the boundaries of traditional gender roles. From the devoted Sita to the fiery Draupadi, these women continue to inspire and empower us even in the contemporary world.

Within the vast world of Indian epics like the Ramayana and Mahabharata, there are some incredible female characters who often don't get the importance they truly deserve. Their voices, stories and perspectives are often overshadowed or pushed aside. Delving into the narratives will seek to understand their struggles, triumphs and the profound impact they had on the mythological landscape. Powerful trio of Sati, Parvati and Ganga to the tragic sagas of Sita, Urmila and Mandodari and the tales of courage from Draupadi, Kunti and Bhanumati will ravel the layers of their stories.

The story of Sati, the first wife of Lord Shiva. Her story teaches us about the power of love and devotion. Despite facing opposition from her father, she chose to marry Shiva and ultimately sacrificed herself to protect his honor. Sati's story highlights the strength and unwavering commitment a woman can possess.

Moving on, to Goddess Parvati, the consort of Lord Shiva. Parvati represents the nurturing and compassionate aspect of the divine feminine. Her story portrays her determination and perseverance in winning over Shiva's heart through her devotion and penance. Parvati's character teaches us the importance of inner strength and the power of love to transform lives.

Another significant female figure is Ganga, the goddess of the holy river Ganges. Her story showcases her purity and divine nature. Ganga's descent to Earth and her role in purifying souls is a symbol of cleansing and liberation. Her tale reminds us of the importance of purity of heart and the power of forgiveness.

Moving on to the Ramayana, the Goddess Sita, the wife of Lord Rama. Sita's character exemplifies loyalty, purity, and resilience. Despite being subjected to numerous trials, she remains steadfast in her devotion and stands as a symbol of strength and righteousness.

In the Mahabharata, the story of Draupadi, who is known for her courage and unwavering spirit. Draupadi's story is one of resilience and dignity, as she faces challenges and stands up against injustice. Her character teaches us about the strength of a woman's voice and the importance of standing up for what is right.

These are just a few examples of the powerful female figures in Hindu mythology. Their stories offer valuable lessons on love, devotion, resilience, and the multifaceted nature of femininity. Exploring these stories allows us to gain insights into the diverse roles and qualities that women embody, inspiring us to embrace our own strengths and potential.

Power of Shakti: Sati, Parvati and Ganga

In Hindu mythology, Shakti represents the divine feminine energy. Sati, Parvati and Ganga are three powerful goddesses who embody this energy. Sati, also known as Dakshayani, was the daughter of King Daksha and the first wife of Lord Shiva. She displayed immense devotion and sacrificed herself in a great act of love. Despite her father's disapproval of their union, Sati chose to marry Lord Shiva and stood by him. Unfortunately, her story took a tragic turn when she sacrificed herself in a fire ritual. This event led to the transformation of Sati into Parvati. Her story is an example of love, sacrifice, and ultimate selflessness.

Parvati, also known as Uma, is the incarnation of Sati, the daughter of Himalaya. Parvati dedicated herself to intense penance to win the heart of Lord Shiva. Her determination and devotion eventually led Shiva to accept her as his wife. Parvati is revered as the gentle and nurturing goddess who embodies love, fertility and motherhood. But there is another facet of her gentle nature, as she also possesses a fierce and powerful aspect known as Kali.

Ganga is considered to be a part of Lord Shiva as his divine consort, forming the powerful duo known as Shiv Shakti. Her association with Lord Shiva symbolizes their divine union and interplay of creation and destruction. She is often depicted flowing from Lord Shiva's matted hair, signifying the descent of divine knowledge and spiritual purity. River Ganga herself is considered sacred and worshipped by millions of people. In Mahabharata, Ganga plays a significant role as the mother of Bhishma, the legendary warrior.

These three powerful female figures represent the essence of Shakti, the divine feminine energy. Together, the stories of Sati, Parvati, and Ganga illustrate the multifaceted nature of Shakti. They exemplify qualities such as devotion, strength, nurturing, and purification. These goddesses inspire us to embrace our own inner power, to be resilient in the face of challenges, and to find balance in our lives.

Sad Sagas of Ramayana: Sita, Urmila, and Mandodri

Ramayana narrates the tale of Lord Rama's journey during the exile. It also highlights the struggles faced by Sita, Urmila and Mandodri. Sita, Lord Rama's wife, is an embodiment of purity, devotion and strength. She faced immense challenges and endured a period of exile and separation from her beloved husband and later for society she was sent to exile again where she played a role of mother living in the hermitage of sage Valmiki.

Urmila, Sita's sister and wife of Lord Lakshmana, showed immense sacrifice by staying behind to take care of her in-laws and fulfilling her duties with unwavering devotion to support her husband Lakshmana during the exile. Urmila is known for selflessness and sacrifice who is often overshadowed by her prominent counterparts.

Mandodri, the queen and the wife of demon, Ravana, also has a tragic tale. She was torn between her loyalty to her husband and her recognition of his wrong doings. Her character showcases the complexities of love, duty and the moral dilemma she faced.

These three women play significant roles in the Ramayana, showcasing different aspects of feminity and strength. These sad sagas of Sita, Urmila, and Mandodari in the Ramayana depict the struggles, sacrifices, and resilience of women. They inspire us to embrace virtues such as devotion, loyalty, sacrifice, and compassion. These characters serve as powerful examples of the strength and grace that women possess, even in the face of adversity.

Tale of Courage in Mahabharata: Draupadi, Kunti and Bhanumati

Mahabharata is filled with tales of bravery. Draupadi, Kunti and Bhanumati exemplify this courage. Draupadi, also known as Panchali, is the central character of Mahabharat. Draupadi faced numerous challenges, including a forced marriage to the five Pandavas and the humiliation while being disrobed by Dushasana on the order of Duryodhana who won the game of dice which later on resulted in the trials of the Kurukshetra war. Despite the hardship, she remained steadfast, displaying unwavering strength and determination.

Kunti, the mother of the Pandavas, showcased her strength as a single mother and made difficult choices for the well-being of her sons.

Despite her husband's actions, Bhanumati, the wife of Duryodhana displayed immense strength, grace and dignity at the time of adversity. She stood up for what she believed was right and showed compassion and kindness towards others. Though a lesser-known character, she exemplifies courage.

These tales of courage in the Mahabharata, featuring Draupadi, Kunti, and Bhanumati, inspire us with their strength, resilience, and unwavering spirit. They remind us of the power of determination, love, and loyalty, even in the most challenging circumstances. These women serve as role models, showcasing the different facets of courage in their own unique ways.

Conclusion

In conclusion, by throwing light on the untold stories of marginalized mythological female characters, we unveil a treasure trove of empowerment and richness. These heroines, often overlooked and overshadowed, embody the very essence of Shakti, the divine feminine energy. Their narratives, woven into the fabric of the Ramayana and Mahabharata, offer us a deeper understanding of their resilience, strength, and wisdom. By celebrating these unsung heroines and acknowledging their invaluable contributions, we not only honor their legacy but also inspire future generations. Their stories have the power to ignite a spark within us, reminding us of the untapped potential and strength that resides in each and every one of us. So let us continue to uplift and celebrate the stories of these remarkable women, for they are a testament to the indomitable spirit of the human experience.

References

- Rao, Gayatri. *Tales of Ramayana: Sita's Perspective*. Chennai: Notion, 2021.
- Anandani, Manini.J. *Mandodari: Queen of Lanka.* New Delhi: Penguin, 2018.
- Manmath. *Sati: the girl who chose the hermit.* Kindle, 2021.
- Chhawchharia, Ajay Kumar. *The Legend of Shiva.* Kindle, Nov 27.2015.
- Chandramouli, Anuja. *Ganga*: *The Constant Goddess.* Rupa, Nov 20. 2018.
- Dasgupta, Karol. *Mandodari: The Sati Series* IV. JULY 03,2023.
- Krishna, Vashmi. Draupadi: India's First Daughter. India: Paper Town, JULY 10.2020.
- Prabhupada, A.C. Bhaktivedanta Swami. *Teachings of Queen Kunti.* Bhaktivedanta, JAN 01.1990.
- Bhuyan, Priyanka. *Chronicles of Kuru Woman- Vol II.* Bigfoot, JAN 01,2021.
- https://www.hinduamerican.org/blog/sita-nature-in-its-feminine-form/
- https://medium.com/@chachamravi/lesser-known-characters-from-indian-epics-urmila-ramayana-3e03b256c445
- https://scroll.in/article/946091/who-was-mandodari-each-version-of-the-ramayana-gives-ravanas-wife-a-different-role-and-story
- https://mythbusterx.wordpress.com/2020/05/30/mind-blowing-story-of-shivas-marriage-with-sati-in-the-heaven%F0%9F%94%A5/
- https://www.indiaforums.com/forum/topic/3985959
- https://booksandyou.in/products/shiv-parvati-a-unique-example-of-love-sacrifice-and-devotional-surrender
- https://www.dollsofindia.com/library/draupadi/
- https://www.mahabharataonline.com/stories/mahabharata_character.php?id=57

12. Transgender in India

Bharti A. Palaspagar
Department of English
R.T.M. Nagpur University, Nagpur
Email ID: bhartipalaspagar1@gmail.com

Introduction

Transgender are those human beings who don't belong to the socially constructed gender and biologically determined sex. The journey of transgender in our society is correlated with marginalization struggles and identity crises. In Indian society they are often seen dressed in ill-fitting blouses and colorful sarees, roaming around the busy marketplace in groups, in the daily local train clapping their hands in a distinctive human voice and asking for money this is the transgender community of India. Trans-phobia is deeply rooted in our society. Isolation and neglect of the third gender deny them of their existence. Acknowledgment of the transgender in our society is the first and foremost step to relieving them of their insecurities. This article is an attempt to trace the journey of transgender in India and study the challenges faced by them. Transgender refers to an individual who has a different gender identity from their biological sex. As an identity, it is called the third sex (tritiyaprakriti) in Sanskrit. This group of people has an internal desire to exercise an opposite external manifestation of social behavior than what is expected from them.

Diversity has been seen in India. People belonging to various religions, languages and cultures are accommodated but when it comes to the transgender community, society does not accept them, and India falls a little short of accommodating them. Marginalization of transgender in India has turned into a creative force. Their autobiographies can be considered as writing back to the center, where the center is occupied by both Eurocentrism as well as mainstream Indian society which still marginalizes and discriminates against trans genders. In India, they are known as Hijras. Transgenders have historical evidence in the writings of ancient India. Transgender of India who have been marginalized and isolated for decades have taken to writing to let their unheard voices echo in the ears of society. There are ordeals to be recognized as more human beings let alone to be treated equally.

Transgender Literature of India change in their attitude to the transgenders of the Nation.

Now the status of transgender has completely been transformed in these contemporary times. This study is an attempt to explore new vistas of the life of transgenders. SathyashreeSharmilais is India's first transgender lawyer. She has become an example to all transgenders. Now she can fight against injustice. She has worked as an activist for the transgender community for more than 11 years. She enrolled her name in the Bar Council of Tamil Nadu and Puducherry. She is from Ramanathapuram district of Tamilnadu. PrithikaYashimi is India's transgender police officer. She is the first trans sub-inspector woman in Chennai, Tamilnadu. She took charge as sub-inspector in Dharmapuri district in Tamilnadu. Shabnam Mausi is India's first transgender MLA. She contested the election from the Sohagpur constitution in the district of Shahdol, Madhya Pradesh.

Naaz Joshi is India's first transgender international beauty queen, she well known as a novelist and critic. She won the Miss World Diversity Beauty pageant three times in a row. Adeline Virginia Woolf is the world's first transgender English writer. She has written the book Orlando and the Waves. She is a novelist, essayist, publisher, and critic. She is from London. Toyota Mondal became India's first transgender person to be appointed as a judge in the Lok Adalat. She has appealed to the government for reservations for transgender communities people in jobs. She now runs her organization Dinajpur NotunAlo (Dinajpur New Light) which works for the welfare of people from the community.

Laxmi Narayan Tripathi is the first transgender to represent Asia-Pacific at a United Nations Task meeting. She has been playing an important role in uplifting the lives of the LGBTQ and transgender communities in India. She is also an actress, a Bharatnatyam dancer, a choreographer, a motivational speaker, and a writer. Laxmi was physically abused as a child. However, coming out of such a situation she fought for the transgender community. Finally, Article 377 makes her optimistic about transgender community's future. But Laxmi think that the change in perception only when she has to initiate it herself. Laxmi NarayanTripathi's "Me Hijra Me Laxmi" is the most popular autobiographical novel. This novel illuminates the struggles and her suffering, memories, and relationships. Third-gender life has affected a person's life. This book reflects Laxmi's plight and her struggle to overcome social barriers.

Living Smile Vidya is an Indian transgender women actor, assistant director, writer, and trans-dalit rights activist from Chennai. She has a master's degree in linguistics and is keenly interested in contemporary theatre and cinema. Living Smile Vidya written Biography "I Am Vidya'' in the Tamil language. This biography was translated in seven languages. Living Smile Vidya was born as men and the family was called Sarvanan. She writes about her journey to be recognized as a woman in her biography. Her inspirational work in Dalit history honors her creative mediums. The story of one such a journey-that of declaration of the claim of identity and acceptance. She had a difficult childhood because of the stern behavior of her father towards her education. That's a really dramatic journey of acceptance of Sarvanan to become Vidhya.

Manabi Bandyopadhyay became India's first third-gender principal at Krishnagar Women's College in Nadia District in West Bengal on 9 June 2015. She was selected on merit for this post. She holds a Ph.D. in Bengali literature. She was an associate professor of Bengali at the Vivekananda Satavashiki Mahavidyalaya in Jhargrame. At present she is the vice chairman of the West Bengal Transgender Development Board, the government of West Bengal, and an executive council member of Kalyani University. Positovartika (Endless Bondge) book is written by Manobi Bandhyopadyay, the book is best seller book in Bengali Literature by their gender. Monobi's childhood was loaded with premonitions of her lifelong struggle with identity and well wishes referring to the family's increasing prosperity and commenting at her birth. She was raped by her cousin in class V and physically assaulted by the boys of her school. She started realizing that she was different but her first memories as a child are those of a boy no different from the other boys of his age. Her story is about the fight for her identity and claiming assertion of her transgenders in society.

Now the societal scenario has changed. Transgenders have educated themselves, acquired high positions, and have written books in English literature including other literature at the global level. The first novel on transgender people was Orlando in 1928 by Virginia Woolf, Gender Outlaws by Kate Bornstein, and Cobra by Severo Sarduy are some of the best and most popular transgender works. Now well known for their achievements they often wonder at how education has created marked differences between the trajectory of her own life and that of the transgender.

References

- Tripathi Lakxmi Narayan. Me Hijra,Me Laxmi. New Delhi:Oxford University Press.2015

- Living Smile Vidhya. I am Vidya. Oxygen Books.2007 Tamil Nadu (India)

- Manabi Bandyopadyay. A Gift of Goddess Laxmi. Penguin Random House India Pvt. Ltd. 2017.

- https://www.ohchr.org/en/special-procedures/ie-sexual-orientation-and-gender-identity/struggle-trans-and-gender-diverse-persons

- https://www.economist.com/open-future/2018/06/29/transgender-identities-a-series-of-invited-esseys

- https://journalsofethics.ama-assn.org/article/transgender-rights-human-rights/2016-11

- https://studycorgi.com/transgender-its-history-and-development/https://www.hrc.org/resources/understanding-the-transgender- community

13. 'किन्नर' खंड काव्य में बयाँ किन्नर जीवन का दर्दभरा यथार्थ

डॉ. सपना तिवारी
एसोसिएट प्रोफेसर
दा.रा.बा. सिंधु महाविद्यालय पाँचपावली, नागपुर
Email ID: profsapna1234@gmail.com

कवि विश्व का ऐसा अद्भुत सृजनकार है, जिसका जीवन परहित के लिए समर्पित है । वह गिरे हुए को उठाता है, रोती हुई आँखों के आँसू पोछता है एवं निराश जीवियों के लिए आशा का दिव्य दीपक जलाता है । साहित्य सम्राट मुंशी प्रेमचंद जी कहते हैं "कवि वह सपेरा है जिसकी पिटारी में साँपों के स्थान पर हृदय बंद होते हैं ।"

वस्तुतः समाज में जो घटित होता है साहित्य में उसकी अभिव्यक्ति होती है । वास्तविकता यह है कि समाज में जो कुछ व्याप्त है, वह साहित्यकार की संवेदना, चिंता और चिंतन का विषय होता है । अपनी कलम से वह अपनी अंतर अभिव्यक्ति और समाज की चिंताओं का साक्षात्कार हमसे कराता है ।

वर्तमान समय की विषम परिस्थितियाँ तथा व्यस्ततम भाग दौड़ की जिंदगी में लोगों के पास लंबी कहानियाँ या उपन्यास आदि पढ़ने का समय नहीं है । उसे तत्काल ऐसा कुछ चाहिए जो उसे जागृत करे । उकसाए, परिस्थितियों की संजीदगी से मिलाए । जिंदगी के कटु यथार्थ से साक्षात्कार करवाए । इसके लिए कविता ही एक ऐसा सर्वाधिक सशक्त प्रभावी माध्यम है जो समाज और समाज से जुड़ी प्रत्येक व्यवस्था चाहे प्रकृति हो या मनुष्य प्रत्येक विषय को कठोरता व कोमलता दोनों ही रूप में यथार्थ अभिव्यक्ति देती है ।

श्री संतोष बादल कवि हृदय होने के कारण उनके अंतर्मन में लोकजन और उससे जुड़ी चिंताएँ अत्यंत व्यापक फलक पर विद्यमान हैं। अब तक उनके 12 काव्य संग्रह तथा 6 खंड काव्य प्रकाशित हो चुके हैं ।

कहा जाता है कि साहित्य ही समाज का प्रतिबिंब होता है और जीवन जितना जटिल और संघर्षमय उहापोह से भरा होता है तो कवि कर्म उतना ही जटिल होता जाता है । काव्य साधना वैसे ही कृच्छ साधना है जिसे एक योगी ही कर सकता है तो दूसरा सम्यक दृष्टा और भोक्ता । ऐसे ही सम्यक दृष्टा कवि बादल जी ने अपनी काव्य रचनाओं के माध्यम से समाज से जुड़ी प्रत्येक पक्ष की चिंता को अपनी अनुभूति व यथार्थता के साथ चित्रित किया है । उनकी काव्यमय अभिव्यक्ति केवल ऊपरी अभिव्यक्ति नहीं अपितु उनके हृदय तल की गहराइयों से निकलने वाली बेचैनी को अभिव्यक्त करती है । यही बेचैनी और अकुलाहट उनके द्वारा रचित उनके सातवें खंड काव्य 'किन्नर' में किन्नर जीवन की वेदना और त्रास बनकर यथार्थता के साथ उभर कर आई है ।

वैसे तो हम सभी जानते हैं कि इस मानव समाज में दो लिंगो स्त्री तथा पुरुष को मान्यता प्राप्त है और इन्हें ही सृष्टि का मूल आधार माना गया है । लेकिन समाज में एक तीसरा वर्ग जिसे सभी लैंगिक विकलांगता या विकृति कह धिक्कारते व ठुकराते हैं । जीवन की घोर निराशा, अपमानित घृणित जिंदगी जीने वाले यह तृतीय लिंगी इस समाज में अपने अस्तित्व के लिए प्राचीनकाल से आज तक संघर्ष कर रहे हैं । तृतीय लिंगी समाज की आंतरिक मनोदशा व व्यथा को बादल जी ने अपनी धारदार कलम से किन्नरों को इस सभ्य समाज में उचित स्थान, अधिकार व सम्मान देने का आह्वान अपने इस खंड काव्य 'किन्नर' में किया है ।

किन्नर शब्द हिंदी के दो शब्दों से मिलकर बना है किं + नर जिसका अर्थ होता है वह नर जो नर होते हुए भी नर नहीं है लेकिन पूर्ण रूपेण नारी भी नहीं है अर्थात जो लैंगिक रूप से न नर होते हैं न मादा ।[1] किन्नर शब्द सुनते ही हमारे मानस पटल पर समाज के ऐसे लोगों की छवि उभर कर आती है जिन्हें समाज हिजड़ा, पवैया, छक्का, नपुंसक लिंग या थर्ड जेंडर के नाम से जानता है ।[2]

सभ्यता के जिस दौर पर मानव समाज खड़ा है वहाँ वास्तव में अपने मानवीय मूल्यों को खो बैठा है । यह अत्यंत लज्जास्पद है कि

संवेदनहीनता, आत्म केंद्रीयता व स्वार्थ के चलते तीसरे वर्ग को जन्म देने वाले माता-पिता ही अपनी ऐसी संतान को हिकारत से देख अपनी जिंदगी से दूर कर देते हैं । किन्नर की तिरस्कृत जिंदगी की व्यथा बादल जी की कलम से कुछ यूँ बयाँ हुई है - "जन्मा कहाँ और किसने पाला किससे पूछूँ कह दे कौन? मेरे इन प्रश्नों पर अक्सर हो जाता समाज क्यों मौन?"

एक ओर आदमी के रूप में मनुष्य को गरिमा से जीने का हक जन्म से मिलता है, जिसे कोई व्यवस्था नीति- कानून छीन नहीं सकता । परंतु समाज की दकियानूसी परंपराओं के चलते इस समाज द्वारा उन्ही जैसा तृतीय लिंगी व्यक्ति समाज से निष्कासित कर दिया जाता है । उसे अलग-अलग एकाकी जीवन जीने हेतु बाध्य कर दिया जाता है ।

"कैसा जीवन कैसा वैभव कैसे अरे उन्माद रहे हम तो इस जीवन सागर के जीते जी अपवाद रहे"
रिश्ते - संबंध जो जीवन को अर्थ, स्थिरता और मकसद प्रदान करते हैं, वहीं रूढ़ियों लोकापवाद, असुरक्षा की दृष्टि से तृतीय वर्ग हाशिए पर धकेल दिए जाते हैं । अपने अस्तित्व की तलाश में ये किन्नर जिन्हें सभ्य समाज व परिवार मनुष्य की गणना तक नहीं देते और कठोर यातनाएँ सहने मजबूर कर देते हैं ।

किन्नरों के समाज से जुड़ी हुई परंपरागत रस्मों का जिक्र भी प्रस्तुत खंडकाव्य में हुआ है, जो कि उनकी जीवन रीति को समझने में सहायक है। इनमें निर्वाण संस्कार का अत्यंत महत्व होता है। यह एक ऐसा संस्कार है जिसमें किन्नरों को पूर्ण रूप से स्त्री बना दिया जाता है।" निर्वाण संस्कार में उस किन्नर शरीर से पुरुष लिंग भेद किया जाता है। इस क्रिया को छिबरना कहते हैं। बिना किसी के चेला बने हिजड़ा निर्वाण नहीं कर सकता। लिहाजा इन्हें मजबूरन चेला बनने तैयार होना पड़ता है। "3
"न मैं नर हूँ न मैं नारी किन्नर का जीवन कैसा? अनचाही मंजिल पाने मिस अंगारों में चलने जैसा"

किन्नर की यही सोच कि मैं एक किन्नर हूँ तो क्या किन्नर होना अपराध है? जो उसे उसके स्वभाव के विपरीत कार्य करने के लिए विवश किया जाता है । क्या एक किन्नर को बधाई देने या ताली बजाने के अलावा अन्य कोई दायित्व नहीं सौंपे जा सकते? किन्नरों की इस वेदना को उद्घाटित कर कवि ने बड़ी ही निर्भीकता के साथ समाज के समक्ष प्रश्न रखे हैं । किन्नर की यह वेदना अंतर्मन को झकझोर कर रख देती है कि मैं किन्नर हूँ तो मुझे क्यों बाध्य किया जाता है कि मैं घर-घर जाकर ढोल बजाऊँ नाचू गाऊँ?

"कब तक करतल ध्वनि करते हम नृत्य करें गलियारों में , कब तक करें प्रदर्शन खुद का गलियों में चौबारे में"

कवि किन्नर के जीवन का उपहास करने वाले सभ्य समाज की यथार्थ तस्वीर को अंकित करते हुए कहते हैं -" हम मानव से पैदा होकर भी मानव न बन पाए, छलते सदा हमें रहते हैं तेरी मानवता के नरू शाए"

"कहाँ दिखी है किसी नयन में, मुझको अपनों से पीड़ा जिसने भी देखा है हमको , चाह रहा बस काम क्रीड़ा ।"

बादल जी ने किन्नर जीवन के दर्द भरे अनछुए पहलुओं को गहरी वेदना के साथ अभिव्यक्ति दी है किस तरह समाज में इनका शारीरिक, मानसिक शोषण, तिरस्कार और अवमूल्यन होता है । समाज का यह वर्ग किस तरह अपने अधिकारों से वंचित है । यह समुदाय मानव विभेद का प्रतीक, इंसानी अधिकारों से मरहूम आमतौर पर सामान्य जन के प्रत्येक शुभ कर्मों की रस्मों से जुड़ा है । लेकिन इनका अपना स्वयं का जीवन शुभकामनाओं, आनंद, आल्हादो से कोसों दूर क्यों है? यह विषय हमें गहन चिंतन के लिए विवश करता है कि कब समाज का यह वर्ग अपने लिए बेहतर जिंदगी, अपने अधिकार, शिक्षा, रोजगार जैसी चिंताओं से मुक्ति पाएगा । बादल जी ने किन्नर की जिंदगी का यथार्थ समाज के समक्ष उपस्थित कर सभ्य समाज के वास्तविक स्वरूप का पर्दाफाश किया है ।

"पहले तो रचकर कुचक्र एक, किया हमें किन्नर विधि ने, रौंद हमारे अधिकारों को, किया नपुंसक फिर तुमने ।"

किन्नर जीवन अवसादों से पटा पड़ा है । खुशियाँ तो उनके लिए मृगतृष्णा की भाँति हैं । हमारा समाज यह समझता है कि इनका जीवन कितना आरामदायक है लेकिन वास्तविकता तो कुछ और ही है इन्हें हर वक्त अपनों से दूरी का गम, तीज त्योहारों में अकेलापन उनके जीवन में नासूर की तरह चुभता है ।

"चाहत है उनके मन में, तात रखेंगे सर पर हाथ पूछेंगे फिर पीर हृदय की, चूमेंगे फिर मेरे गात"

अपने जन्मदाता से एक किन्नर का अत्यंत मर्म स्पर्शी प्रश्न है - "जब बनना था संबल तुमको, तात मेरे मेरा जग में, छीनी राहें मुझसे मेरी, तुमने ही मेरे पग से?"

सभ्य समाज की सबसे बड़ी विडंबना है कि उन्हें यह भली भाँति ज्ञात है कि किन्नर से किन्नर का जन्म नहीं होता यह इस सभ्य समाज की ही देन है । स्त्री पुरुष से ही इनका जन्म होता है । पर वह इन्हें अपना नहीं पाते आखिर ऐसा क्यों? किन्नर का किन्नर रूप में जन्म लेना ही बेहद दर्दनाक और पीड़ा दायक है । कैसे-कैसे हालातो का उन्हें सामना करना पड़ता है । किन्नर रूप में जन्मा बच्चा जिसको यह ज्ञात नहीं होता है कि वह क्या है? मासूमियत में लिपटा है फिर भी समाज उसको हैवानियत भरी नजरों से देखता है । कवि का समाज के प्रति दुष्कर प्रश्न कुछ इस तरह सामने आते हैं -

"बजा - बजाकर करतल अपने,
हम जीवन निर्वाह करें
कृत्य तुम्हारा या उस प्रभु का,
हम क्यों उसका मूल्य भरें?"

"तेरा ही रक्त वीर्य हूँ,
फिर भी ऐसी बदहाली,
तेरे चेहरे पर है लालिमा,

पीट रहे हैं हम ताली?"

"है जिनमें जननांग वही केवल मानव है?
जो विहीन उससे क्या वे केवल दानव है?"

किन्नर जीवन की एक ज्वलंत वेदना है कि वह जन्म तो पुरुष रूप में लेता है और पूर्णत विकसित नहीं होता परंतु उसकी भावनाएँ व विचार स्त्री से मेल खाते हैं जो बड़ा होकर विवाह कर सामाजिक व वैवाहिक जीवन निर्वाह करने में असक्षम रहता है । उसके जीवन का यही सबसे बड़ा दंश है।

"किन्नर हूँ नर बन सका नहीं, न नारी सी प्रतिमा पाई
मेरे जीवन में तो बस मेरी, पीड़ा ही हरदम मुस्काई"

'किन्नर' खंडकाव्य किन्नर समाज के बहिष्कृत जीवन का वह लेखा-जोखा है जिसमें किन्नर द्वारा सभ्य समाज से यही याचना की जा रही है कि उन्हें तृतीय लिंगी या किन्नर नहीं बल्कि इंसान समझा जाए क्योंकि उसकी देह रचना भी मानव सृदश है । उनकी रगों में भी लाल रक्त बहता है फिर भी वह समाज से बहिष्कृत क्यों है?

"हम दिखते तो मानव सृदश पर, कहाँ हमें मानव माना, तिल - तिल हम मरते रोज रहे, जीवन क्या हमने क्या जाना?

बादल जी ने 'किन्नर' खंडकाव्य में किन्नर जीवन की बदहाली को बड़े ही साहस, सशक्तता के साथ अभिव्यक्त किया है । पुस्तक का एक-एक पद दिल की गहराइयों को छूकर मन को द्रवित कर देता है और किन्नर के जीवन की बदहाली को समझने, उसे इस दलदल भरी जिंदगी से उबारने की शक्ति व प्रेरणा प्रदान करता है ।

किन्नर समाज भी यही चाहता है कि उनका जीवन बेबस लाचारी भरा न हो । उन्हें भी इस मानव समाज की दुनिया में इंसान समझा जाए । उनकी बस इतनी सी माँग है कि वह भी समाज की मुख्य धारा से जुड़ना चाहते हैं । शिक्षित होना चाहते हैं । देश के विकास में अपना

योगदान सुनिश्चित करना चाहते हैं । कवि भी समाज से उनके जीवन के लिए यही अपेक्षा रखते हैं-

"शिक्षित बनो ज्ञान अर्जन कर, नव प्रभात के खोल दो द्वार, आज दिखा दो सकल सृष्टि को, नहीं अरे हम हैं लाचार "

"तज दो सब नैराश्य हृदय का, ऊँचे आदर्श बनाओ तुम कितना कूतुहल है तुममें, जग को आज दिखाओ तुम"

सारे दुखों, अवसाद, पीड़ा विपरीतता, विषमता के बावजूद कवि ने आशा के दामन को नहीं छोड़ा । आशा के प्रदीप को जलाए चलो को अपने खंडकाव्य में सार्थकता प्रदान की है । 'किन्नर' खंडकाव्य में बादल जी ने किन्नर की सर्वत्र आशा, विश्वास, स्वप्न, अरमान और संभावना को अंतर्मन से अभिव्यक्ति दी है । उनकी यही सोच है कि रात जितनी काली घनी होती है, सुबह उतनी ही उजली और रंगीन होती है । अतः कवि की आशावादी दृष्टि से यही परिलक्षित होता है कि एक न एक दिन किन्नर को उनका स्थान, सम्मान, अधिकार अवश्य मिलेगा । वह अत्याचार नहीं सहेगा । अपने अस्तित्व की लड़ाई में वह सम्मान पूर्वक अपना अधिकार लेकर रहेगा । साथ ही प्रस्तुत खंडकाव्य में यह संदेश निहित है कि मानव समाज के लिए यह बेहद जरूरी है कि वह किन्नर की बुनियादी आवश्यकताओं को समझे, उन्हें अपनाए । उन्हें उनका हक व स्थान प्रदान करें । हमें उनके प्रति उदार और सहिष्णु होना होगा, उनकी अस्मिता व अस्तित्व को स्वीकारना होगा ।

अतः स्पष्ट है बादल जी की प्रस्तुत कृति युग, समाज और किन्नरों के अंधकार नैराश्य जीवन पर चिंता ही व्यक्त नहीं करती अपितु समाज के ठेकेदारों से सीधे कटाक्ष कर टकराती है और उसके भाव सकारात्मक परिणाम की आशा भी करते हैं । प्रस्तुत खंडकाव्य में किन्नर जाति का अपनी अस्मिता व अस्तित्व बनाए रखने की आकांक्षाओं को पूर्ण करने का आक्रोश ध्वनित होता है । जन्म से लेकर मृत्यु तक वह निरंतर केवल सहते हैं और जब भी प्रतिरोध करने की चेष्टा करते हैं उन्हें समाज द्वारा बेरहमी से कुचल दिया जाता है । किन्नर के जीवन को जिस बारीकी   और बेबाकी के साथ बादल जी ने अपने शब्द बाणों

की वर्षा की है वह स्तुत्य है, सराहनीय है । बादल जी ने शब्दों के साथ खिलवाड़ नहीं बल्कि कुशल शिल्पी की भाँति उन्हें अपने हृदय के तारों से मोती की तरह पिरोया है । कवि का कृति के कला पक्ष और छंद विधान पर पूर्ण अधिकार है । भाषा शैली की सहजता, संप्रेषणीयता और सरलता जो पाठक को अपने साथ सिर्फ बाँधे नहीं रखती अपितु विषय को गहनता के साथ सोचने, समझने के लिए बाध्य भी करती है ।

'किन्नर' खंडकाव्य किन्नरों के प्रति एक प्रेरणात्मक आह्वान और किन्नर जीवन की दुरूहता यथार्थता पर अंकित उसका एक - एक उद्बोधन क्षितिज पर होते अरुणोदय, उषा के आने की आहट और किन्नर जीवन को ऊर्जा प्रदान करने वाले भास्कर के आगमन का सूचक है । काव्य गरिमा से मंडित बादल जी की प्रस्तुत कृति जहाँ कथ्य और अभिव्यक्ति से सशक्त है तो दूसरी ओर संवेदना और भावनाओं से सराबोर अभिव्यंजना मानस के मन को झकझोर देने वाली है। यह अद्भुत कर्म एक सच्चा साधक सर्जक ही कर सकता है ।

प्रस्तुत कृति किन्नर समाज की व्यथा को समझने तथा तृतीय लिंगी समाज की बदहाली को वाणी देने में बादल जी वाकई कामयाब हुए हैं। बादल जी ने 'किन्नर' खंडकाव्य पुस्तक के माध्यम से किन्नरों की ज़िंदगी से खिलवाड़ करने वाले सभ्य समाज की यथार्थ तस्वीर को हमारे समक्ष रखकर इस विषय में गहन चिंतन के साथ संवेदना व्यक्त करने हेतु आह्वान किया है।

संदर्भ

1. देवी मोनिका 'अस्तित्व की तलाश में सिमरन' , माया प्रकाशन, कानपुर, 2019, पृ. 9

2. मेहरा, दिलीप, 'हिंदी साहित्य में किन्नर जीवन' , वाणी प्रकाशन, दिल्ली, 2019, संपादकीय

3. अक्षरवार्ता मासिक अंतरराष्ट्रीय रेफर्ड जरनल, दिसंबर 2017, भाग 2, पृ. 68

4. महेंद्र, भीष्म, 'मैं पायल' , अमन प्रकाशन, कानपुर, 2016, पृ. 75

5. बादल, संतोष, 'किन्नर' खंडकाव्य, ज्ञानमुद्रा पब्लिकेशन, भोपाल